Betrayed by God?

Making Sense of Your Expectations

Shana Schutte

BEACON HILL PRESS

OF KANSAS CITY

This book is dedicated to four strong women in my family who know how to ride the roller coaster of life and still hang on: my mom, Hazel Schutte, who is one of my greatest confidants; my amazing grandmother, Freda Nicholson, who always inspires me to keep looking ahead; my sister, Melonie Schutte, who has learned to go after her dreams no matter the cost; and my lovely sister-in-law, Jeana Schutte, who knows what it's like to experience loss and still have the courage to love. I am so blessed to have all of you in my life. Thank you for loving me!

This book is dedicated also to my mentor, Cheryl Mitchell, who taught me how to press into Christ when I felt abandoned and betrayed by God.

Contents

1. When Dreams Die   9

2. Feeling Betrayed Creates a Bigger Mess   23

3. Disconnected from God   35

4. Making Unhealthy Vows   47

5. Trading God for Something—or Someone—Better   61

6. Feeling Betrayed by God Leads to Sin   73

7. Trying to Make God in Your Image   89

8. Sometimes It Looks as If God Doesn't Care   103

9. Heartbreak Creates Questions You Can't Answer   119

10. God's Motives Can Be Mysterious   135

11. Heartbreak Can Threaten Your Relationship with Christ   147

12. Does God Care Enough to Make You Whole?   161

13. Getting Back to God   175

Acknowledgments   188

1
When Dreams Die

*Life is not predictable, except in its
unpredictability.*
Dan B. Allender, *The Healing Path*

God: The most popular scapegoat for our sins.
—Mark Twain

Little girls know how to dream. Ask any elementary-school cutie patootie what she wants to be when she grows up, and she'll probably give you a list as long as her list for Santa.

I picked up my friend's five-year-old daughter, Alyssa, from school one afternoon. As acting mother, I did what moms often do—I engaged her in conversation.

"How was your day?" "How was lunch?" "How did you like gym?" Then I asked another common question: "What do you want to be when you grow up?"

A dreamer, this sweet little thing with legs dangling over the back seat of my car unloaded dreams, hopes, and desires for her future at machine gun speed without taking a breath. "I want to be a ballerina, and I'm gonna play the clarinet, and I'm gonna do house stuff and play the piano and be an artist, and I'm gonna be a scientist and do math, and I'm gonna be a teacher, and I'm gonna be a writer and play the flute."

"House stuff," I discovered, meant actually building houses and giving them to the poor—a daring goal for such a tiny girl. Yes, little girls definitely know how to dream.

So do big girls.

Think about it. When you meet your girlfriends for a night out, how long is it before you're all going on and on about what you long for? If you're like me and my friends, it's about five minutes.

Every dream, hope, or desire we have resides on what I call an internal checklist of the heart. Just like Alyssa, we started keeping this personal list when we were little, adding to it through junior high, high school, and into adulthood. Sometimes we add things to the list, sometimes we take things off, but there's always a list. Sometimes we don't even know what's on it until God doesn't grant us something we want or we're unpleasantly surprised by something we haven't put on the list.

No one gets everything on the list; life rarely turns out exactly the way we want it. Our days on earth are a series of little disappointments over our lifetimes. We want a new couch, but we're stuck with the one our grandmother recovered with her old drapes. We want a promotion, but we receive a demotion. We want our children to get better grades, but they don't.

And then there are bigger things on our lists that, if left unchecked, deeply wound our longing hearts: We want intimacy, but we're misunderstood. We want health, but we become ill. We want fidelity, but some of us are traded in for newer models. We want children, but we're childless. We want stability, but we're faced with unemployment. We want acceptance, but we're snubbed by a family member. We want to be faithful, but we succumb to unfaithfulness. We want to overcome an addiction, but we struggle with it in spite of our prayers.

And then we experience disappointments that happen to us corporately. We want our nation to prosper, but its prosperity is threatened by a growing load of debt. A hurricane destroys our homes and the homes of our neighbors. Hardships surround us.

Life is never easy. Thus, the items on our internal checklists are never entirely checked off.

Yvette Maher knows what it's like to have something big remain unchecked on her list. On January 7, 2008, Yvette's twenty-year-old single daughter came home and told her mom that she was pregnant. Yvette was shocked, of course. As director of a sanctity-of-human-life organization, she and her husband had done everything possible to educate their children about God's plan for sex. For three days Yvette stayed home and supported her daughter, working out the details of how to handle this family crisis.

On January 10, while preparing to stop by Starbucks on her way to work, Yvette received a phone call from her sister. "I need you to pull over," she said. Yvette braced herself for unhappy news. "Dad has been accused of shooting his girlfriend," she said. "He's fled the scene, and there are dogs and helicopters looking for him. The whole county is in a lockdown. You need to get here. But you need to know that when the police find him, they'll probably shoot him. So be prepared."

As Yvette hung up the phone, she began preparing herself for the worst. She raced home, threw a suit into a bag, called her family together to explain the situation, then drove sixty miles to the Denver airport.

That night around 9 P.M. she arrived in Lexington, Kentucky. Shortly after landing, she discovered that her father was in the hospital, but due to strict legal guidelines and because her father was already a convicted felon, she couldn't get any information on his condition. The district attorney told her that she would need a court order to see her father—no exceptions.

Three days later she entered his hospital room. She was shocked by what she saw. Instead of the police having shot him, he had tried to kill himself. Half of his face was gone, including his right eye, ear, and cheekbone. He looked like a character in a horror film.

Yvette stood over her father. *I can't believe this is happening,* she thought. *My daughter's pregnancy and now this.* Her dad had already been in jail for ten years after being convicted for murder. But since his release two years earlier, he and Yvette had been rebuilding their relationship. Now what?

Ten months later, her father was sentenced to life plus ten years in a Kentucky prison.

At the end of the same year Yvette and her husband, Tommy, felt the strain of the crises on their relationship. "We hit a major wall of exhaustion and spiritual depletion. It was like 'I don't know if I like you, love you, or can't stand you,'" Yvette said. The Mahers considered separation but later worked out their differences with the help of a licensed counselor.

Within twelve months, Yvette's daughter had became pregnant, her father had shot his girlfriend and was sent to prison for a second time, her marriage almost fell apart, and her beautiful grandson was born.

When I asked Yvette if she felt betrayed by God, her eyes widened, and she replied, "You know what's crazy about all this? In all the troubles I've experienced, I feel as if God is the only one who *hasn't* betrayed me!"

Do you feel like Yvette? Blessed in spite of tragedy? Loved by God in spite of some extremely difficult circumstances?

Or—as I have—have you felt that God has let you down, betrayed you?

I'll never forget when I pounded my bed crying and screaming, *God, I hate you!* On that day in 1992 everything significant I had believed about myself, God, my relationship with Him, and His teachings seemed to die under the heavy weight of disappointment.

My heartbreak was excruciating, because it centered on a woman's most intimate longing—romantic love. Like most women, I wanted to become a bride more than anything. Convinced that life would be unbearable if I couldn't marry the man I loved, I pleaded with God to let me have him. In complete seriousness I asked, *Lord, if I never get married, would you please let me die?* The fact that I said that to God should have warned me that my desire was so all-encompassing that there could be an intense and dangerous reaction in me if He said no.

I prayed kneeling, crying, begging, standing, sitting, and screaming, but the man I longed for married someone else. A subsequent four-year spiritual and emotional black hole sucked me into enemy territory where Satan had what my mother calls a "heyday." I was in such emotional pain that I could no longer understand who God was or who I was to Him.

Because He didn't give me what I wanted, I believed He had betrayed me, leaving me in a spiritually and emotionally messy place. If this is your story, you know that there are few things more painful.

Why did *I* feel God had betrayed me in *my* circumstances, yet Yvette didn't feel that way? My troubles could be considered small compared to hers. What spiritual perceptions hindered my walk with God while Yvette's walk with Him grew stronger in spite of what she endured? Why do some people see their houses burn to the ground and sail through trouble with flying colors of faith? Why do others experience something that seems as small as having a hangnail and end up hating God?

In *The Sacred Romance* John Eldredge writes,

> Everyone has been betrayed by someone, some more profoundly than others. Betrayal is a violation that strikes at the core of our being; to make ourselves vulnerable and entrust our well-being to another, only to be harmed by those on whom our hopes were set is among the worst pain of the human experience. Sometimes the way God treats us feels like betrayal.

Ah, yes. It *feels* like betrayal. But is it?

Are our perceptions wrong if we believe God has betrayed us when life hurts? Do we have some faulty expectations about God, ourselves, our relationship with Him, and the Bible? Are we confused about His heart and intentions toward us?

Have we been deceived?

Perhaps reading my story reminds you of a personal wound that caused you to ask God questions you've been afraid to whisper to Him in the dark, let alone speak out loud. Maybe you weren't jilted on your way to the altar, but your experience has been equally painful. Your heartbreak may have happened when you were an adult or when you were young. Maybe it caused you to scream at God, as I did, or maybe you expressed your pain more politely. Nonetheless, there has been a time when you've questioned His goodness and love and have felt that God has betrayed you.

If you or someone you know relates to the experience of feeling betrayed by God in some way, there are a few things you need to know before we begin to examine that reaction.

Feelings of betrayal require honesty with God.

Being honest with God about the ugly things in our hearts doesn't always come easily. Many believe that it's *not* okay to say we're angry with God or that we feel He's lied to us, let us down, or betrayed us. Right? We've been led to believe that messy emotions are not okay and that being honest about our doubts is spiritual taboo—that "Hallelujah!" and "God is good!" should be constantly on our lips.

There's a better way.

When we're brokenhearted due to loss or disappointment, God wants us to be honest with Him. Why? Because being truthful creates an open door for Him to walk through to heal us. That's the way grief works. When we let it out, He comes in to apply His healing truth to the places that hurt.

One day it hit me afresh that the Psalmist did this very thing. Then I unexpectedly got the idea to do something I used to do when I was in the second grade—color in my Bible. I picked two of my favorite hues: pink and green. Every phrase in which the Psalmist expressed feelings, I highlighted pink. In the places he proclaimed God's truth, I colored the words green. The result was an interesting pattern: Pink, green. Pink, green. Pink, green. Feelings, truth. Feelings, truth. Feelings, truth.

This reminded me that God shows that His plan for my life involves the blending of my emotions with His truth. One without the other never brings emotional healing or keeps me from believing the lie that God has betrayed me.

What if a woman lives only according to her feelings? There will be no healing for her broken heart, because emotions alone are often untrustworthy and can be based on lies. But what if she acknowledges only God's truth and stifles her emotions because "It's the Christian thing to do"? Healing remains elusive, because she's living a life of denial about what's really going on in her heart.

God wants to merge what we *know* in our heads about His Word with what we *feel* in our hearts, even if it means admitting some ugly things such as that we're angry with God, believe that He's lied to us and let us down—or that He's betrayed us. It's only when we're honest that He can change our song of betrayal to a song of joy.

Faith requires that we live not just from our heads but also from our hearts. Only then can faith be transforming. This means that I allow God to touch the messy places of my internal life; I engage my emotions and cooperate with God to blend them with His truth.

I recently had the privilege of speaking with Ruth Graham, author, speaker, and the third child of Billy Graham about being honest with God. When Ruth married at the age of eighteen, she believed marriage was for life. "I made a pact," she said, but when she learned that her husband of twenty-one years had been having multiple affairs, she was disillusioned with God.

This wasn't supposed to happen to me. I used to think that if I did this or did that or the other, God would bless me. But then, when something bad would happen, I struggled with disappointment, and I was angry with God. I stood on God's promises that He would do a new thing in my marriage, thinking that He would improve things, but then I realized that He was doing a new thing in *me* instead.

Part of the "new thing" God did in Ruth in the aftermath of divorce was to teach her how to cultivate greater intimacy with Him through honesty.

Now I see God as gracious and welcoming. I imagine myself talking frankly with Him, crawling up into His lap, and saying, 'All right, this is how I'm feeling.' God wants us to be honest. He wants to include us, not exclude us in any way. He handles honesty very well. We can be open with Him and talk to Him like a friend.

God wants your honest feelings when you are hurting from not getting something you longed for. If you continually suppress the monster of disappointment, it will continue to raise its ugly head again and again. God can't heal what you won't give to Him, and denial will keep you bound by feelings of betrayal.

God wants you to surrender what you don't understand.

I used to think that I couldn't get past believing God had betrayed me or come to trust Him again unless He explained why my heart was broken and why I didn't get what I wanted. I've since learned that surrendering to Him is necessary to overcome any distrust I feel. And it does not require that He reveal anything to me about my past disappointments. He's not obligated to tell me why my heart was broken or why someone else has experienced the joys in life that I've longed for. Rather, in surrendering I'm giving up what I don't understand to a God who loves me.

Because of this, I can choose to believe moment by moment that He's sovereign over every detail of my life—and all things in my past, present, and future.

In *Just Enough Light for the Step I'm On* Stormie Omartian writes,

> God wants us to surrender our dreams, because we can't be led by Him if we are chasing after dreams of our own making. And He wants us to surrender all of them. That way He can tell us which of them are from Him and in line with His will and which of them are ours and born out of our will. If they are only our dreams and visions and not His, we will experience a lifetime of unfulfillment and strife trying to make them happen.

Can you relate? If so, count yourself in good company. I've often wondered why we're so slow to let go. I believe one reason is that we doubt God can give us anything greater than what we desire.

Trusting and surrendering to God does not mean that it will always feel nice to give up to God what we don't understand. Neither does it mean always skipping and singing hallelujahs through our troubles. Instead, it may often mean that we say, "I trust you, Lord," through tears, through shouts of despair, and possibly even through clenched teeth—because trust and surrendering to God are a choice, an act of the will not born of emotion.

I'm still single at age forty-one. Remaining unmarried has been my deepest heartache, because—like most women—a loving husband and family have been important items on my checklist. Although I've felt capable of giving and receiving love for many years now, the wedding altar has eluded me.

God and I have had many talks about my still being single. In some of my most personal moments with Him, I've raised my hands to heaven with tears streaming because I don't have a man to love or a child to hold, and I've surrendered to God: *Lord, my life is yours. You know what's best for me. If I can serve you best alone, then I do it willingly.*

I've chosen to surrender to Him many times when the longing of my heart is fierce. There's no doubt that remaining in God's hand is not always an easy thing, *but it's always the right thing.* I think about eternity and the people I want to take with me to heaven. I think about the souls I want to touch for Christ. And for these reasons I trust Him because these "light and momentary struggles" (2 Corinthians 4:17) will be outweighed by the glory of eternity. I say yes to Jesus. I agree to go His way.

If you feel betrayed, you're in the majority.

Some time ago, I e-mailed 125 women and asked them if they had ever felt betrayed by God. Ninety-eight percent replied that they had.

If you identify with these women, I congratulate you on your honesty. You're already on the way to discovering a deeper love for God and healing for your heart. It's my prayer that He'll speak to you through this book.

If you've never felt betrayed by God, you have good reason to believe that many of your friends are in the 98-percent who feel they've been. Hopefully this book will fuel your compassion, love, and understanding as you walk with them through difficult circumstances.

God wants to run circles around your checklist.

One of my friends recently said, "The search for satisfaction always ends in the same place; it always ends in God." I wish I had known that before I believed God had betrayed me; I wish I had known that God was going to run circles around my checklist.

This truth is illustrated in Matthew 5:4—"Blessed are those who mourn, for they will be comforted." The word "blessed" in this verse is *makarios* in the original Greek language, and it refers to the state of the believer in Christ. The definition from my New Testament word study Bible says, "He (the Christian) is indwelt by God because of Christ and is *fully satisfied*" (emphasis added). The thing that strikes me most about this definition, however, is the remainder of the definition: "*Makarios* differs from 'happy' because 'happy' describes the person who has good fortune."

Don't you love that? This means that no matter what items on your list have or haven't come through, you can experience satisfaction. And unlike me, you can avoid the mess that's sure to develop once you begin believing that God is a betrayer.

If you can relate to my story because you believed that something or someone could satisfy you in a way that Christ couldn't, and that led to feeling betrayed by God, I invite you to remember *makarios*.

Examining Your Heart

1. What's your greatest dream, hope, or desire?

2. What if anything do you desire that would cause you to feel as if God didn't love you or care for you if you never received or achieved it? Would you feel betrayed?

3. Is it difficult for you to share your ugliest emotions with God? Why or why not?

4. Why do you think it's difficult to surrender to God what you don't understand?

5. Do you agree with Stormie Omartian's belief that we have to give up all our dreams to God so that He can give back those that are of Him? Why or why not? Would this be difficult for you to do?

6. How does it make you feel to know that God could want something for you other than what you desire for yourself?

7. Have you ever experienced the satisfaction of *makarios* in spite of your circumstances?

Action Point

Draw a heart on a sheet of paper, and write in it the dreams, hopes, and desires you hold most dear at this time. Then draw another heart, and write inside it the dreams, hopes, and desires you valued ten years ago. Has your list changed? Can you see God's wisdom in withholding some of the things you wanted ten years ago?

2
Feeling Betrayed Creates a Bigger Mess

I always think of my sins when I weed. They grow apace in the same way and are harder still to get rid of.

—Helena Rutherfurd Ely, *A Woman's Hardy Garden*

You have wearied the LORD . . . by saying . . . "Where is the God of justice?"

—Malachi 2:17

Have you noticed that weeds never stay in one spot? They aren't happy taking over just a skinny crack in the sidewalk; they have to dominate the whole thing. They won't stay in the corner of the garden—they have to rule it. They choke out flowers, bushes, and berries. Left to run rampant, all that's beautiful will become victim to the nasty things.

I recently spoke with a friend who said, "I think I'll go to my church and help weed the yard." She began her task early in the day to avoid the summer heat. She wore her gardening gloves and a smile. *This will be an easy job—an hour will do the trick,* she thought.

Boy, was she surprised!

The lunch hour came and went, and she was still yanking up a network of nasty thistles. The root system was like a super-highway shooting out here and there all over the yard. Her hands were blistered. Her back ached. She was frustrated, having been pricked and punctured by all sorts of pokey and sharp things. What started out as a simple job became a burden. Why?

Because the weeds had taken over.

When we feel betrayed by God, our hearts are like gardens that have been taken over by weeds. And like the weeds in my friend's churchyard, they come to rule. These weeds aren't content to stay in one little corner of your heart—they want to take over your entire life. This is critical to remember, that feeling betrayed by God is not just a harmless emotion. In fact, if these betrayal weeds are allowed to take root, they'll destroy everything beautiful in your heart.

How does that happen? How can feeling betrayed by God produce something so insidious that it wreaks havoc in your whole life? Let's start by taking a look at how betrayal weeds grow.

Betrayal weeds grow out of roots, just like regular weeds.
Have you noticed that *everything* grows from *something* and that *nothing* comes from *nothing*? A tree grows from a seed, love grows from respect, a good painting grows from good talent, and love grows from God.

Believing that God is a betrayer grows from something, too. In the same way a tree grows from a seed and love grows from respect, betrayal weeds always grow from roots of deception.

Always.

Roots of deception are lies. When a woman doesn't get something on her checklist and believes that God has betrayed her, she has allowed at least one—and likely more—of Satan's roots of deception to grow in her heart. These are Satan's lies, because he's the father of lies (John 8:44). For example, she may believe that God doesn't love her, that He's a liar, unfair, or a celestial bully. Any of these lies could cause her to feel that God has betrayed her when life hurts.

I watched a documentary on television on the beautiful late Farrah Fawcett that detailed her battle with cancer. In one scene she was speaking with her father, and he said he was praying for her or, as he put it, "talking to the man upstairs" and asking Him for healing. Farrah asked her dad why God doesn't always answer prayer—and her dad replied that sometimes God is just too busy.

Too busy? What woman can trust a god who's so busy he ignores her and not powerful enough to manage the affairs of the world?

In 1967 seventeen-year-old Joni Eareckson Tada dived off a rock into shallow water, broke her neck, and became a quadriplegic. She also believed that God was too busy and that He had abandoned her. Joni thought that just as she was getting ready to dive into the water, God had become distracted with someone else's problems and turned His back. Thankfully, Joni is now a trophy of God's grace and a shining light of His love.

Late author C. S. Lewis believed a different lie about God after his wife's death. At the time, he chronicled his painful feelings in a very transparent book titled *A Grief Observed*. Lewis didn't believe that God was too busy but rather that He was cold and distant:

> Meanwhile, where is God? A door slammed in your face, and a sound of bolting and double bolting on the inside. After that, silence. . . . There are no lights in the windows. . . . Why is He so present a commander in our time of prosperity and so very absent a help in time of trouble?

Any of these lies—God is too busy, cold, or distant—or others could lead a woman to believe that God has betrayed her when circumstances spin out of control.

When I believed God had betrayed me, I didn't struggle with the belief that He was too busy, cold, or distant. I felt He was *indifferent* to my heartache. I knew He had the power to intervene, but He didn't. From my perspective, He simply didn't care enough to get involved in my personal affairs. I even had some crazy idea that He cared enough about me to die for my sins so that I could go to heaven, but that was it. Eternity was His priority—not the heartbreak I was experiencing in the here and now.

The Five Categories of the Roots of Deception

I once took inventory of the roots of deception I believed had convinced me that God had betrayed me. I discovered that they weren't all just about God or His character. Instead, they fell into five primary categories:

1. **Lies about God**
2. **Lies about me**
3. **Lies about my relationship with Him**

4. Lies about what the Bible says

5. Any combination of the above lies

In my life these categories included the following roots of deception. Can you relate to any of them?

- God doesn't hear me when I pray.
- God doesn't love me.
- God hates me.
- God is punishing me.
- I'm a bad person.
- I'm not worthy of love unless I'm good.
- God's love for me is passive—He's not actively involved in my life.
- God doesn't want to provide for my needs.
- God loves other people more than He loves me.
- Some parts of the Bible aren't true.
- God won't protect me when other people hurt me.
- God never gives me what I really want.
- God lied to me.
- Being a Christian doesn't work.
- No one loves me.

With roots of deception like these buried in the soil of my heart, it's no wonder I felt betrayed!

Your ability to reject roots of deception will determine if you live victoriously despite disappointments or if your heart becomes overrun with betrayal weeds. The only defense against deception is God's truth.

Unbelief in God's love is a common root of deception. Believing in His love is critical to guard against feeling betrayed. When we're confident of God's love, we can rest securely in Him when life hurts. The hard part is that believing He loves you doesn't mean you won't experience disappointment or heartache. It means that you'll run *toward* God rather than away from Him when your life gets messy.

Betrayal weeds give roots of deception the appearance of being true.

When I was a girl, I had a "deception-appearing-true" experience I'll never forget. I was seven when my older sister and I heard that a circus was coming to our little town in southern Idaho. We couldn't wait. When the big day finally arrived, we walked to the high school football field a half mile away, found a seat high on the bleachers, and waited for the show to start.

I don't remember anything about the circus except for one terrifying incident. Part of the way through the show, the animal trainers rolled out a large male gorilla in a cage. When one of the men carefully opened the enclosure to free the animal, I was fascinated. Just as I stretched my neck around the girl in front of me to see what might happen, the gorilla jumped over the chain-link fence and ran up the bleachers. Children shrieked and scattered as he ran straight for me.

Wide-eyed and terrified, I darted away just in time. I didn't know what happened to my sister, and I didn't care—I just wanted my mom. I'm also not sure how I got to the street below, but I do remember running as fast as I could all the way home.

As it turned out, it wasn't a gorilla at all. It was just a man in a gorilla suit. But it serves as a good example of circumstances that can validate the lies we believe. I believed the gorilla was real, and the lie was validated by what I saw: a big, hairy, snorting beast that ran like a gorilla.

When we face deep disappointment or loss or physical challenges or any number of the difficulties of what life sometimes brings, if we're not careful and knowledgeable, we can begin to believe one or more of the five lies. When that happens, Satan will make sure that something will occur to validate those lies—the roots of deception that lead to feelings of betrayal.

That's what happened to Sharon. Although she had walked with God for many years, she didn't believe He cared about her marriage. The root of deception was buried deep in her heart.

One day Sharon came home and found her husband with another woman. Because the lies she believed *appeared* to be true based on her circumstances, she shouted, "Just what I thought—God doesn't care about my marriage!" Immediately, she believed that God had betrayed her—because she accepted this root of deception as truth.

Sometimes when a woman is caught in the throes of deep disappointment, grief, or loss, Satan will *suggest* a lie—a root of deception—when her heart is crushed, thus causing her to feel betrayed.

Proverbs 14:15 says that only a simpleton believes anything. In the same way, we can't always believe everything we see. When circumstances cause the lies we believe to *appear* to be true, it's time to grab hold of our faith and God's understanding, because this is how a wise woman lives. A wise woman also relies on the truth of what God says about himself in the Bible, regardless of the circumstances that cause us pain. Always believing what we see battles against faith.

A perceived injustice grows from the roots of deception.

After a woman embraces one or more roots of deception, suffers a disappointing setback to the life she was expecting, and her circumstances appear to validate the lies she believes, the betrayal weed will continue growing unless it's eradicated with God's truth. Then she'll pin the perceived injustice on God. I say "perceived," because it only *looks* like injustice. This is part of Satan's plan to deceive.

One of my coworkers sent me a true story of a Romanian prisoner who sued God and, like Sharon, pinned the injustice on Him. As I read it, I didn't know whether to laugh or cry, but I was certainly struck by its irony. "God received different material valuables from me," he said, "as well as prayers in exchange for promises of a better life. In reality this did not happen."

Because of good deeds and childhood baptism, the man was convinced that God was legally required to protect him from the devil and give him what he wanted, not unlike what many offended believers have demanded in their own relationships with God.

This man believed his imprisonment was proof that God hadn't held up His end of the deal and had acted unjustly. He demanded that the Romanian Orthodox Church, which the plaintiff considered to be God's earthly representative, compensate him for "God-inflicted damage." The lawsuit was thrown out because it was determined that God is "not subject to a civil court of law's jurisdiction." Duh!

Taking God to court sounds absurd, of course, but don't we often define God's justice by what does or doesn't happen in our lives? We put Him on trial because He doesn't deliver what we've dreamed for, hoped for, or desired. Even if we don't verbalize it, we sometimes think, *If God is just, He'll give me a new job. If God is just, He'll allow me to have a child. If God is just, He won't allow me to suffer financial difficulties.*

We have no idea that we believe God is unjust in any way until we don't receive something we want or we get something we didn't want. I doubt that this prisoner-plaintiff determined that if he ever went to jail he would blame God. But when he was looking out from behind bars, the lies he truly believed about God and God's justice surfaced. Ultimately, because he was not secure in God's love and faithfulness and because he was prideful, feelings of betrayal and a trivial lawsuit followed.

Condemning God is nothing new. In Job 40:8 God asks Job, "Would you condemn me to justify yourself?" It is written of Job's faithfulness, "In all this [suffering], Job did not sin by charging God with wrongdoing" (Job 1:22). In God's book, blaming and condemning Him are sin.

Furthermore, if we *condemn* God and put Him on trial, we'll suffer double. We experience grief when we lose our dreams, hopes, or desires, but we'll also suffer because feeling betrayed keeps us from receiving Christ's comfort and peace when our hearts are broken.

Betrayal weeds have taken over when a woman charges God with an injustice.
Remember: weeds come to take over. I've read that a single weed can produce more than 10,000 seeds. Like the weeds did in my friend's churchyard, a betrayal weed spreads thousands of seeds throughout a woman's heart and produces lots of offspring.

These offspring wreak havoc in a woman's life and can produce bad feelings that cause her to believe that God has betrayed her.

It's important that we take inventory to determine if any of the following seeds are planted in our hearts: doubt, bitterness, hardness of heart, pride, vows, fear, hopelessness, lack of peace, guilt, covetousness, envy, idolatry, prayerlessness, self-righteousness, indignation, desperation, loneliness, or rebellion.

In upcoming chapters we'll focus on three of these seeds—hardness of heart, vows, and idolatry.

When we experience any of these feelings, it does not necessarily mean that we believe God is a betrayer. I've experienced loneliness, guilt, and fear without believing that He has been unfaithful. However, if we allow betrayal weeds to grow unchecked, we can be enticed into sin that leads to ruin.

It's much better to get to the problem of the root of deception when we're disappointed and heartbroken. And God's truth is the ultimate deception-destroyer! As Ruth Graham once told me, "There's no substitute for grounding yourself in Scripture."

God's love is like a beautiful weed. One afternoon I was speaking with a good friend about betrayal weeds. She said, "God's love is like a weed, too—a beautiful one that spreads out and takes over our lives, not through force but through surrender. God isn't a bully—He gently woos us with His love. When His beautiful love spreads throughout our hearts and takes over, we know we haven't been betrayed, regardless of what life circumstances we face."

There's no broken heart that God cannot heal, no hardness of heart that He cannot soften, no fear, guilt, or other betrayal seed that He can't eradicate from the heart of one who is willing to choose to believe Him.

Examine Your Heart

1. What spoke to you most in this chapter?

2. What roots of deception named in this chapter do you relate to most? Why? Are there others not listed in this chapter that Satan has used to hinder or destroy your relationship with God?

3. Has there been a time in your life when you've pinned a perceived injustice on God because circumstances made God look guilty? Has God changed your perspective?

4. Has there been a time when circumstances caused something to *appear* to be true that later you discovered to be false?

5. If you've felt betrayed by God, what betrayal seed did you struggle with most?

Action Point

List the roots of deception that you identify with most. Then talk with God about each one, and ask Him to show you His truth. Don't hesitate to get out your Bible and find scriptures that contradict each lie that has fed these roots of deception. You may want to write the truth about each scripture on a note card and carry it with you to meditate on during times of doubt about God's love and faithfulness.

3
Disconnected from God

God is not what you imagine or what you think you understand. If you understand, you have failed.

—Augustine

To put one's trust in God is only a longer way of saying that one will chance it.

—Samuel Butler, *Note-Books*

Minutes before my grandfather passed away, my sister and I stood at the end of his hospital bed holding hands. As I prayed for Grandpa, my heart whispered, *Run home [to heaven], Grandpa! Run home!* I was glad that my heart hurt, because it meant I wasn't just breathing in and out. My emotional pain revealed that I had the capacity to love. When I believed God had betrayed me, I felt just the opposite. My heart was hardened, and I wondered some days whether I was dead or alive, but I always knew I wasn't free.

Hardness of heart is one of the results of feeling betrayed by God. It creates an emotional numbness that makes it difficult to feel pain or joy or to love deeply. Most tragically, it also makes us deaf, blind, and unperceiving to the things God wants us to know and understand. It robs us of the abundant life He intends for us.

When we live with hearts that are hardened toward God, we may realize we're not living life to the fullest, but we may also feel that it beats opening our hearts and risking more emotional pain. Hardening our hearts is not the way to heal what hurts.

God takes hardness of heart seriously.

Parents usually instruct their children most in the areas of life they (the parents) take most seriously. In Hebrews 3:7–4:7 God is described as a good father who repeats important instructions to his kids. He's so adamant that the Israelites not harden their hearts toward Him that He warns them against it three times in eighteen verses. He drives home the point—and He wants us to get it too.

In Mark 8:17-18 Jesus said to His disciples, "Do you still not see or understand? Are your hearts hardened? Do you have eyes but fail to see, and ears but fail to hear? And don't you remember?"

In these verses Jesus sets out for us the symptoms of a hardened heart: the inability to see, the inability to understand, the inability to hear, and the inability to remember.

How do we know if we have a hardened heart? We have an inability to perceive "God stuff." The heart is a commander, and the senses follow the heart's lead. Once the heart is hardened, the senses follow suit. If the heart is soft, the senses will be open, pliable, and receptive. If the heart is hard, the senses will be hard also, making it impossible to see and hear God. One's entire ability to discern good from evil and to understand God's ways are destroyed by hardness of heart.

Where there's hardness of heart there's also deceit.

In Hebrews 3:13 God says that where hardness of heart is, deception is always present. Smoke goes with fire, calories go with cheesecake, and lies go with hardness of heart. Sometimes we harden our hearts as a means of self-protection, sometimes because of pride, rebellion, fear, or anger. But whatever the reason, where hardness of heart is, there's *always* deception.

Several years ago during a difficult season, I felt my heart begin hardening against God. Then I remembered that I was allowing myself to be deceived. I knew that I had to remain pliable to God to avoid Satan's schemes. I looked up "deceit" in the dictionary and discovered that "delusion" is a part of deception. Because hardness of heart involves deceit, it's simply not grounded in God's reality.

When we struggle with a hardened heart toward God because of loss or disappointment, it's important to revisit the roots of deception (listed in the last chapter) and ask God if we're believing a lie about Him, about self, about our relationship with Him, about the Bible, or a combination of two or more of the first four lies.

Hardness of heart prevents the perception of love.

"Do you still not see?" (Mark 8:17).

I once read an article about a man who said he always knew that he and his wife were meant for one another but never realized how much until one day while reminiscing about their childhoods.

They had been chatting for a few minutes about the old days when the man discovered that both he and his wife had visited the White House during their elementary school years and that both remembered having their photographs taken with the president. No doubt this was a joyful surprise, but it was nothing compared to the delight they experienced when the man pulled out an old box of photos from his trip to Washington, D.C., to find the two of them standing shoulder to shoulder in the photo with the president. Wow! Two kids in the presence of true love—and they didn't even know it at the time.

Hardness of heart causes us to block out God stuff that we should be taking in—like truth, direction from the Holy Spirit, and love. Even when we're smack-dab in the presence of love, even when we're standing right next to it, and even when it died on a cross, we still can't see it.

It's like a couple who've had considerable strife between them. They've been arguing for several months, and the tension has been building. The wife holds a grudge against her husband. Rather than choosing to forgive, hardness of heart controls her so that every little thing he does is filtered through this hardness.

One night as he starts to rub her back before bed because he wants to her to feel loved and accepted, she becomes angry because she believes that he just wants to use her for sex and his own gratification. The next day when he sends her flowers, she thinks he's trying to manipulate her, when nothing could be farther from the truth.

It can be the same way with God. Along comes the loss of a job, and rather than believing God wants to help us through it, we believe He's punishing us. We develop a physical problem, and hardness of heart leads us to believe that God doesn't care, when in reality He loves us deeply.

Hardness of heart destroys or hinders communication with God.

"Do you still not . . . understand?" (Mark 8:17).

In his book *The Sacred Romance*, John Eldredge tells a story about a time in high school when he fell in love with a beautiful sophomore named Joy. One day, several months into the relationship, he was thumbing a ride home from school when he saw Joy whiz by in her convertible with another guy. John wrote, "I felt the fool, which we often do when we feel betrayed. And I never gave my heart again."

When we feel betrayed by God and harden our hearts, we may vow never to be vulnerable to Him again. So we lock the tender, wanting part of ourselves away from Him, and we stop praying. We believe that this is best, because then He won't have the power to hurt us anymore through the vulnerability that transparent prayer creates.

Or maybe we don't completely stop talking to God. Instead, we develop a shallow prayer life that lacks substance. We throw up "cotton-candy" prayers in traffic, in the shower, or as we run out the door to go to work. This way we can stay on the safe side of petition by asking God for things that haven't really captured our affection and pose no risk of disappointment. This allows us to feel that we've done our duty to pray even though we're convinced that God has been unfaithful, and we no longer really trust Him to hear us.

Let's call it *"praying* it safe."

When I developed a "cotton candy" prayer life, I demanded that my existence be pain-free, and I traded adventure with Him for the mundane. Sure, I got to live in a spiritual safety zone, but I also forfeited the excitement of walking with God in exchange for something easier and less threatening. I traded faith for fear, which meant my heart didn't heal, and full relationship with Him was not restored.

Life with God was meant to be lived in faith. And even if we don't always get what we want, we were created to live on the cliff edge of daring prayer.

What kind of prayers have you been praying lately? Are you sending up "cotton candy" prayers because you've hardened your heart toward God? Have you made a vow that you would never make yourself vulnerable in prayer again, because the last time you prayed for something you felt that God let you down?

Hardness of heart causes deafness.

"Do you have . . . ears but fail to hear?"(Mark 8:18).

The instruction and counsel of God can be spoken to us through the Bible, someone close to us, our circumstances, or the Holy Spirit. Unfortunately, the woman who has hardened her heart toward God can't hear His instruction from these sources, because hardness of heart has made her deaf.

When I felt betrayed by God, I didn't want to listen to Him through Scripture because I felt that it had been a major reason I was hurt. I wrongly thought that God had made promises to me from the Bible that never came to pass. As it turns out, it wasn't the Bible that hurt me but my *interpretation* of it that wounded me. I would often see it on my nightstand and think *I should really read that,* but I didn't pick it up. I didn't want to hear God's voice, because I believed that opening my heart to Him again meant risking disappointment—and I thought that was more than I could bear.

Hardness of heart causes spiritual amnesia.

"Don't you remember?" (Mark 8:18).

Several years ago I met a young man who developed amnesia after someone dowsed the inside of his new truck with gasoline and set it on fire. For reasons the doctors couldn't explain, the trauma from this event caused him to forget many things—including his fiancé. Because he couldn't remember her and the memories they had created together, he also lost the affection he had for her. He forgot that he had once stared into her eyes, held her hand, and exchanged looks of affection. He didn't remember he loved her.

A similar thing happens when we feel betrayed and our hearts become hardened. We develop "spiritual amnesia," and we forget God's truth, our history with Him, and His love for us. But remembering God's faithfulness is a powerful antidote for feelings of betrayal and a hardened heart.

Counselors often tell couples with troubled marriages to reminisce about their early romance, because it stirs up the embers of love to help heal their relationships. This same exercise can renew our relationship with Christ.

For several years I've wanted to collect a pile of small river rocks, wash them, and then write key words and a date on each one to remind me of an answered prayer or a "God moment." Then, when I'm sad or disappointed or I'm tempted to believe that God has been unfaithful, I can pull out a rock to remind me of a special experience with my King—and I could fall in love with Him all over again.

Unfortunately, I haven't gotten around to collecting the rocks, so I use my journal to help me remember His goodness. I recently wrote a note to God after recalling some of my story with Him:

Knowing you has been the most exhilarating, painful, beautiful, difficult, lovely, desperate, treacherous experience ever! We've lived a grand adventure, haven't we, God? Sometimes I've felt that my heart would burst from pain, and other times I've felt it would overflow with so much song that I couldn't stop singing. Life with you has all the elements of a great love story or an on-the-edge-of-your-seat movie. Life with you is an adventure worth remembering.

In Psalm 77:1-10, while experiencing heartache, Asaph momentarily forgets God's faithfulness instead of remembering His goodness. With gut-wrenching honesty, he asks, "Will the Lord reject forever? Will he never show his favor again? Has his unfailing love vanished forever? Has his promise failed for all time? Has God forgotten to be merciful? Has he in anger withheld his compassion?" (Psalm 77:7-9).

Finally Asaph's faith returns, and his heart softens when he writes, "I will remember the deeds of the LORD; yes, I will remember your miracles of long ago. I will meditate on all your works and consider all your mighty deeds" (Psalm 77:11-12).

Even during desperate disappointment, Asaph *chose* faith over believing the lie that God had betrayed him. As a result, he experienced hope, peace, and acceptance instead of a hardened heart.

I've been encouraged when reading a remembrance of God's goodness I've recorded in my journal. Even those of us who don't have long histories with God can turn to others when we're in need of encouragement. Many times I've called on a trusted friend to share her stories of God's faithfulness with me. Without exception I've also come away with increased faith and gratitude.

Hardness of heart toward God and hardness of heart toward others are closely connected.

It's important to note that when we harden our hearts toward God, it's unavoidable that we'll harden our hearts toward others. It also follows that when we harden our hearts toward others, our hearts harden toward God on some level. The two always go together. That's why it's critical to forgive others in order to keep our love relationship with God vibrant and healthy.

I'm not making light of the pain of rejection and conflict, but all relationships carry risk, and there are no guarantees. However, Christ created us for relationships in which grace is given and grace is received. In spite of past experiences, to believe that all men, women, or church people are untrustworthy is a lie of Satan. He wants to rob God's gifts from our lives. (See John 10:10.)

Can you imagine what Christ's life on earth would have been like if He had hardened His heart out of self-protection rather than give His all to those He loved? After being mocked and spurned by political groups, old and young men, and legalistic Pharisees, He would have hardened His heart, made vows about who He would and would not associate with, and what He would say in His final hours on earth. Rather than keeping His mouth shut when He was falsely accused, He would have defended himself. When His enemies spit in His face, He would have retaliated. When they called Him names, He would have called down a legion of angels to defend himself. When they marched Him to Golgatha, He would have fled. Rather than laying down His life, the redemption of the human race would have been lost due to His hardness of heart and self-protection.

When we harden our hearts in self-protection, not only do we miss out on seeing, understanding, hearing, and remembering "God stuff," but we also cut ourselves off from others. As a result, we miss out on being a gift to people, and we ruin our own opportunity to receive the healing God wants to bring to us through others. The redemption of our hearts and the hearts of others will always be hindered because of hardness of heart.

Examine Your Heart

1. What did you read in this chapter that touched you most deeply?

2. Have you developed a "cotton-candy" prayer life or completely stopped praying to God altogether because you feel betrayed by Him?

3. What are some long-term consequences of ceasing to listen to God through His Word?

4. Why do you think hardened hearts leave us vulnerable to spiritual amnesia?

5. Have you ever hardened your heart toward God because of a grievance someone committed against you? Have you forgiven that person so you can experience full relationship with God?

6. What are some of the things you can see, hear, understand, and remember that God has done or is doing in your life to show you His love?

Action Point

Collect some small river rocks and clean them. Write key words and the date on each one with a permanent marker to remind you of an answered prayer or a "God moment." Then place the rocks somewhere in your home where you can easily access them. When you're sad or disappointed, pull out a rock to remind you of a special experience with Jesus. If you don't have any rocks, make a list in a journal, or draw rocks on paper and label them. When you're finished, praise God for His goodness, and talk with Him about your history with Him.

4
Making Unhealthy Vows

Feed your faith, and your fears will starve to death.

—Author unknown

Courage is not the absence of fear, but rather the judgment that something else is more important than fear.

—Ambrose Redmoon

As a veteran Royal Family Kids Camp summer counselor, I was confident I would skate past the trouble so often discussed during our pre-camp staff training sessions, so I shrugged off the camp social worker's warning: "Your camper might become emotionally distant or even volatile toward the end of the week, especially if she feels a special connection with you." Sure, I knew the campers' abusive backgrounds often caused some challenging behavior, but I didn't think it would affect me.

I envisioned my fifth-grade camper, Lisa, and me holding hands, singing songs, making crafts, and talking about Jesus. But as the week unfolded, the social worker's admonition boomeranged and slapped me in the face. Lisa, who up to then had been a delight, started screaming at me at the top of her lungs: "I hate you! I wish you were never my counselor!" I was stunned. *What had I done wrong?*

I searched the campground until I found my mentor, Cheryl. As she had many times before, she set me straight.

"Shana, don't you remember what you learned in pre-camp training? Lisa loves you, and she's pulling away because she doesn't want to get hurt when she has to say goodbye." Lisa, unaware, did what many of us do when we experience a broken heart: She made an unhealthy vow. It was probably something like—*Everyone always leaves me, and it hurts when I have to say goodbye. So I'll just hurt her first before she hurts me.* Her vow was an effort to protect the place where she felt most vulnerable—her heart.

At the time, I didn't have a clue about the relational devastation that would come into Lisa's life if she didn't let go of her vow. But I was even more clueless about a vow I had made several years earlier that was stealing the love right out of my own life. I also didn't know that my vow wasn't just words spoken in a moment when my heart had been broken—it was an agreement I had made with Satan.

Devastated from losing the relationship (mentioned in the first chapter) I had hoped would lead to marriage, I lay in bed and cried until I hyperventilated. My sobs became a wail that catapulted toward heaven and then seemed to hit the ceiling. *God, do you even hear me?* Then I shouted a phrase that changed my life for the next six years: "I'm never allowing any man to get close to me again!" Like Lisa, I didn't want to hurt again, because I didn't think I could handle it. And because I felt that God had betrayed me, I believed I had to protect myself.

Many years later I realized that my vow did, in fact, guarantee that I wouldn't feel the devastation of a broken heart, but it also made sure that I would never experience the joy of God-given love again, because self-protective hearts *can't* love.

The *American Heritage Dictionary* defines a vow as "an earnest promise that binds one to a specific mode of behavior." I thought the vow I had made protected me, but in reality it was binding me. Like a rope that strangles, it had tied itself around my heart until I couldn't feel or express romantic love.

I learned to live from my head, because my experience had taught me that emotions can't be managed and can't be trusted. I made relational rules beyond what was reasonable. I had an over-active intellect and a gun-shy heart. I lived from my head and deprived my heart of its voice. When I sensed love welling up from my within me, I bolted—sometimes physically but always emotionally.

I would take out my mental marking pen and draw boundary lines around my heart. *Now this is safe.* I didn't understand what I was doing or that the vow I made was driving my behavior. But those close to me could see it clearly even if they couldn't verbalize that I had made a vow. Even my mother said, "I see you—you keep guys at arm's length."

I longed for a man to love me, and I even prayed for someone special to come into my life, but because I was self-protective and had stopped trusting God with my heart, I got safety and self-sufficiency instead of love.

Can you relate? Have you made a vow that's robbing the blessings from your life? Maybe it wasn't a man who broke your heart, but perhaps you've vowed never to get close to any women because your best college friend betrayed you, which made you believe that God had betrayed you and let you down. And it felt like more than you could take. Perhaps you grew up with a mother who made sure to tell you every day, "You're stupid." The vow? *I'll never go to college because I can't cut it.* Maybe you never let your husband see you cry, because when you were a child your father always made fun of your tears.

Making such a vow is one of the seeds of betrayal that we talked about in the second chapter. When a woman doesn't get a dream, hope, or desire she was counting on, and she feels betrayed by God, she can make vows about husbands, boyfriends, siblings, children, parents, neighbors, friends, jobs, money, illness, secrets, sins, or anything in between. The reasons for making an unhealthy vow are as different as the women who make them, but all are related to one thing—self-protection. Every time a vow is uttered from the lips of a woman and she buys into it, it binds itself around her heart and robs her of the abundant life God intends for her.

Why does making an unhealthy vow result in being bound? Because these types of vows are closely connected with deception—Satan's favorite method of tying the Christian heart in knots.

Avoid making unhealthy vows.

Imagine this scenario. After searching for many months, Cindy, a new Christian, found a church home, which was a desire of hers. Just as she began to feel at ease in the congregation, a woman from her Sunday School class gossiped behind Cindy's back. Immediately Cindy believed a lie—*I can't trust anyone, not even Christians.* When she accepted the deception that she can't trust anyone, she made a vow: *I'm never going to get involved in church or allow any Christians to get close to me again!*

What led Cindy to make such a vow? Disappointment and a broken heart plus deception.

Cindy's vow robbed her of what God wanted to give her: loving, nurturing relationships in the Body of Christ. As long as she accepts the deception, she is bound, and the results are devastating. The destruction from this vow will spread into many areas of her life and poison her heart and relationships. This betrayal seed begets other betrayal seeds.

Because lies are a part of the equation that led to Cindy's vow, we could write Satan's name above the word "deception." Ultimately, when Cindy accepts the deception, she accepts Satan's agenda for her life. We must search our hearts to see if we've made agreements with Satan by believing his deceptions.

It's important to make a special note about the deception that's part of this vow-making equation. Lies often travel in packs. The above example shows that Cindy's vow was related to one lie, but this is not how it usually shakes out in the life of a brokenhearted woman. For example, in relation to the vow I made for not allowing a man to get close to me, God has uncovered and set me free from at least three related lies that supported my vow and kept me bound.

Vows are an effort to protect ourselves and make up for what we don't believe God will do for us.

My friend Kathleen lived a portion of her life on the street and in foster families. Without the steady presence of a loving mother and father, orphan mentality became a way of life for her. One day as we chatted over coffee, she said, "I realized no one was going to take care of me, so I would have to take care of myself." Her comment reminded me of a friend I made in Africa.

I had packed my luggage with anticipation and suspected it would be exciting ministering to Kenyan orphans with Buckner Orphan Care International. I was right. I experienced many firsts: my first safari, my first flight across the African desert in an airplane the size of a Cracker Jack box, my first time to eat ostrich, and the first time I ever wanted to bring a little girl home whose parents had died, probably from AIDS.

Before the trip, one of my friends prayed, *God, please help Shana connect with just one child.* God answered with a bubbly, six-year-old named Edith whose smile could light up the darkest African night. She didn't need to speak English, and I didn't need to speak Swahili. We spoke with our eyes and our hands and through laughter—which translated into the language of love.

During our last day together, our ministry team prepared to say goodbye to Africa, the orphanage staff, and the children. As the kids loaded their belongings onto the bus, I noticed little Edith carrying two five-pound packs, one on her back and another on her front. She trudged along, grunting under the weight. I ran to catch her.

"Edith! Edith! Let me help!" I expected her to immediately drop her load with the sound of my voice and wait for assistance. Instead, she looked at me, smiled, but kept walking, determined to make it to the bus without collapsing.

I reached down for one of the backpacks, but she insisted on carrying them alone. I realized that this is what Edith's life had taught her: *No one is going to take care of me, so I'll just have to take care of myself.*

My heart broke. Isn't that often the cry of a wounded woman who feels betrayed and abandoned by God? *God, I've prayed and have asked for your help, but you haven't come through. If you aren't going to take care of me, I guess I have to take care of myself.*

When I vowed never to allow any man to get close to me again, I believed that God had dropped the ball—He should have protected me. *If God isn't going to protect me, I guess I just have to do it myself*—orphan mentality followed by a vow.

Have you ever felt as Kathleen and Edith and I felt? Have you ever tried to carry the weight of a broken heart all alone because you believed the lie that God was somehow unfaithful? Have you ever felt like an orphan?

In John 14:18 Jesus says, "I will not leave you as orphans; I will come to you." In the King James Version the word for "orphans" is translated as "comfortless." When you feel as if there's no comfort for your broken heart, God wants to remind you that you're not alone in spite of how you feel.

The vows we make are an effort to do for ourselves what we believe God won't do. We try to be god of our own lives.

When we make vows, we try to manage our own brokenness and either heal or numb the emotional agony we feel. In short, we try to be our own god. And that leads to nothing but multiplied pain.

Scripture tells us that the person who tries to be her own god by lighting her own path "will lie down in torment" (Isaiah 50:11). On the flip side, we can experience comfort from a God who's always willing and able to carry those He loves through their times of brokenness.

God takes the emotional pain of His children very personally, so much so that He dwells with the person whose heart is breaking. (See Isaiah 57:15.) That means that He's more than just a visitor—He "camps out" with us when we're hurting and stays to provide the healing we need. But like Edith, when we make vows, we attempt to carry our own burdens. And that means we can remain stuck in a place of emotional pain much longer than necessary.

Making vows hinders the healing of a broken heart.

Sandy was certain her relationship with her mother was over. Another argument erupted, words were carelessly spoken, and emotions were trampled on. With tears flowing freely, Sandy stomped out of the house, slammed the door, and found a quiet place to fume. *Now I can duke it out with Mother, and she won't be able to argue back!* She spewed a monologue in which she said everything she felt, knowing there would be no consequences.

"Mom, I've decided that I'm not going to love you anymore—in fact, I don't even care if *you* love *me*," she said.

Two things happened during Sandy's "confrontational monologue." One, she made a vow—*I'm not going to love you anymore*—and two, she denied her true desires—*I don't even care if you love me.*

What Sandy didn't know was that when she denied her true desire for a healthy relationship with her mother and buried it beneath a vow, hardness of heart crept in, and healing of her broken heart was hindered.

When we make vows because we feel betrayed by God, we shut Him out of giving us the healing we need. It's like slapping a hand over a bloody bullet wound and telling the surgeon, "No, I can take care of it myself." As a result, God, the Great Physician, is not allowed into the place that hurts. Vulnerability is always necessary for healing, and heartbreak is always buried beneath unhealthy vows that are made for self-protection.

One evening I engaged a young twenty-something waitress in conversation. I asked the question many women are curious about: "Are you married?"

She rolled her eyes dramatically and responded, "Oooh! Been there. Done that. Never doing it again." I'm sure her smile would have convinced a casual onlooker that she wasn't bothered by her painful experience, but I knew otherwise. Why? Because a heart that's healthy, whole, and unbroken has no need to make vows for self-protection. Heartbreak was buried beneath this lovely woman's vow. Undoubtedly, she had also denied any desire she had for companionship, perhaps to the point that she was fully convinced that she longed for no one.

God-honoring vows are a part of His design.

Not all vows are bad. Some are God-honoring. For example, making the vow to love a spouse "for better or for worse" is part of God's design for marriage. A vow to "train a child in the way he should go" (Proverbs 22:6) is God-honoring and supported by Scripture.

One day as I chatted with a small group at a women's retreat, one of the participants said, "A God-honoring vow is one that draws you closer to His plan for your life, and an unhealthy vow made for self-protection draws you away from His will." But is it possible to make a vow, believing that it's faith-filled and God-honoring—when it's really built on self-protection? Absolutely.

Prayer vows sometimes look like faith but aren't.

Several years before I vowed never to allow any man to get close to me again, I made a vow that I would get involved in a romantic relationship only if I knew it was God's will. My inaccurate logic went like this: *I was hurt because I was out of God's will. Now I won't be hurt if I follow God's plan, so I'm going to make sure that I do exactly what He wants.*

My response was to prostrate myself in prayer and make a prayer vow: *God, I won't do anything you don't want me to do. I will involve myself only in relationships I absolutely know are of you.*

I looked for signs and prayed like mad, certain that if I arranged my personal life well enough, I wouldn't experience heartbreak. Is it an expression of faith to ask God to write an answer in the sky? It depends upon the posture of the heart. In situations in which someone is fearful enough to make a prayer-vow like the one I made, to ask God to remove all doubt may not be a sign of faith but rather evidence of a lack of it. Additionally, there may never be enough evidence or "sky-writing" for a fearful woman to move forward with confidence.

Sometimes, in situations in which clear direction is not found in Scripture, such as which job to take or whom to marry, God might ask you to walk by faith and not by sight without writing in the sky.

As you pray and read His Word, He'll ask you to trust that He's working in your circumstances and heart and guiding you even though you don't hear Him speak or see Him write the answer in your Cheerios. There are times when God asks that you be like a toddler who doesn't always worry about taking the next step because she knows her daddy has her hand.

These prayer vows that look like faith can happen when we're considering becoming involved in a new church, purchasing a home, or starting a new career.

I recently spoke with a young man who said that he needs to know with absolute certainty that the woman he intends to marry is "the one." If he's operating out of fear, will he ever have enough faith, even if God is prompting him to marry? Perhaps his vow looks like faith but is really a cover for fear.

Get free by identifying the deception and believing the truth.

Perhaps now you're saying, "Shana, this chapter describes me! I've made a vow, and I know I've bought into some deception. But now what? How do I get free from this unhealthy vow?"

I'm so glad you asked.

Remember the vow-making equation? Disappointment and a broken heart plus deception equal a vow.

When you're ready to get free from the binding power of any vow, you must replace the deception with God's truth. This may mean going back to the root of the problem and identifying roots of deception and get right with God before the vow can be destroyed.

For example, if Bob makes a vow not to attend college because he believes the lie that he would fail and wouldn't be able to handle failure, he'll need to replace the deception with the truth for him to get free. Why? Because deception is the glue that holds unhealthy vows together.

Bob will also need to identify any fears he has that support the vow. For example, he may fear that if he fails, he'll look like an idiot in front of his family. Once he's identified the lies that he can't succeed and that he won't be able to handle it if he fails, and accepts and believes the opposite truths—that he can succeed with God's help, and that he can handle whatever happens with God's help—he'll be free from the vow.

Because we can make vows as children and not realize what we're doing, it took several years for me to understand that I was bound. God showed me that I believed lies that had contributed to my vow, but I couldn't identify all of them. I also recognized that I needed to know the truth to be set free. Above all, something inside me told me that I couldn't liberate myself, that it had to be a God thing. To His praise, one day God promised He would set my heart free, and that's exactly what He did.

Over time God revealed that I feared not being loved and that several lies were feeding my vow never to get close to a man again:

1. That God had betrayed and abandoned me earlier in my romantic life and that he wouldn't help me in a new relationship.
2. That I didn't have the ability to love and be loved.
3. That I couldn't handle another heartbreak.

Somewhere along the way I went from distrusting God and believing He had betrayed me to trusting Him. After that, I was ready to receive His truth. He showed me that I'm complete without a man's love and that He's with me even if I never marry; that He has never left me, even in my most heartbreaking moments; that I have the ability to love and be loved; and that I can handle any heartbreak no matter how difficult.

When I learned *and* believed these truths, my debilitating fear of rejection disappeared—and so did my vow never to get close to a man again.

My heart was finally free! For the first time in years, I had full confidence that I could love without feeling terrified, and a huge weight was lifted from my heart.

Even though I would have liked it to be otherwise, it wasn't an overnight transformation. It took lots of prayer, counsel from the Holy Spirit and a trusted friend, and exposure to the truths in the Bible for the vow to lose its binding power.

Remember this: freedom from unhealthy vows happens only when we accept God's truth. Sure, we can *know* truth, but to be free we have to *believe* truth, to apply it to deception. This comes from being in a loving relationship with God. This means that if you feel betrayed by Him and as a result you've turned from Him, your first step toward healing from any unhealthy vow is to ask Him back into your life.

Examine Your Heart

1. What do you feel God wants you to learn from this chapter?

2. Have you ever made a vow because you felt like a spiritual orphan and didn't believe that God would help you? If so, what circumstances led to the vow? What scriptural truths can you find to combat the lie that God has orphaned you and that you have to deal with life alone?

3. If you've made an unhealthy vow, what was your motivation? For example, fear of being hurt by _____, fear of not being in control of _____, fear of settling for _____, fear of losing _____.

4. How does it make you feel to know that God dwells with you when your heart is broken? (Isaiah 57:15). Think back to your greatest heartbreak. What signs do you have that God was there?

Action Point

To get free from the binding effect of an unhealthy vow, one needs to acknowledge the deception (the glue) that's holding the vow together. If you've made an unhealthy vow, start a conversation with God and ask the Holy Spirit to show you the lies that are holding your vow together. Then, ask Him to show you His truth to destroy the lies. Remember that it will most likely take time, as God renews your mind, to get completely free from the vow.

5
Trading God for Something—or Someone—Better

We know that an idol is nothing at all in the world and that there is no God but one.
—1 Corinthians 8:4

He feeds on ashes, a deluded heart misleads him; he cannot save himself, or say, "Is not this thing in my right hand a lie?"
—Isaiah 44:20

It is insanity to run from God and search for love.
—Erwin Raphael McManus, *Soul Cravings*

During a recent season of heartache, I considered getting something I wanted at the expense of obeying God, because an ache in my heart was pushing me to the edge of obsession. For a few days I believed that fulfilling my desire would relieve my longing in ways that God couldn't. I'm thankful that I took my feelings to God through journaling. He used my journaling to set me straight and reminded me that He alone is enough.

May 21, 2009

Every now and then, my faith is washed away in a torrential downpour of longing. In this stormy ache, everything I have learned about you, who you are, remembrance of what you have done in my life, and the truth of your love for me is washed away in a flood of desire for satisfaction—for something or someone that promises to put an end to my longing. In these moments, when I have forgotten you, when I don't believe you are enough, I am most vulnerable to compromising what I believe, of laying you on the altar and killing my relationship with you for my own dreams, hopes, and desires I believe will satisfy.

Dreams, hopes, and desires such as love, intimacy, romance, children, sex, comfort, companionship, and significance. When these things dominate me, and I feel that I must have them to save me, it's because I doubt that you are enough.

Doubting you, doubting your love, the doubt beckons me to trade you for an idol, a lesser love. But if I let you go, what do I have? Like the Psalmist, I ask, "Whom have I in heaven but you?" Who in all of earth, all of my city, all of my home, and all of my bed at night? Whom have I but you? No one. No one compares.

No, I will not kill my relationship with you by exchanging you for an idol, a lesser love, for my greatest love is you. I will not trade you in for temporary satisfaction. You last forever. Idols and lesser loves do not.

Have you ever thought that if you could just have something or someone you desired that you could be more satisfied than you are with God? Have you ever wondered if another love or desire could take His place, that something or someone else could save you from life, fear, loneliness, desperation, heartbreak, disappointment, or any other ailment of heart?

When a woman feels betrayed by God, one reason is because a dream, hope, or desire has become an idol—it has trumped Christ. She thinks it can somehow give her something God can't. Unfortunately, this idolatry creates a domino effect that leads to chasing and embracing even more idols. For this reason, idolatry is one of the causes, but also the seeds—or results—of believing God is a betrayer. When a woman romances an idol because she feels betrayed by God, she's like a woman who cheats when she feels that her husband isn't meeting her needs.

Here's a short quiz to help you determine if something you desire has become an idol.

- Does what you want trump God?
- Is your allegiance directed toward your dream, hope, or desire instead of God?
- Do you worship or love your dream, hope, or desire instead of God?
- Do you obey or serve what you want instead of obeying or serving God?
- Do you believe that getting what you want will save you, but God can't?
- Do you believe that you can't live without your dream, hope, or desire?
- Have you walked away from God because He hasn't granted what you dream of, hope for, or want?

Are you convinced that something or someone you want has become an idol, or do you feel you're giving God enough of your life?

I recently received an e-mail devotional written by the late pastor Adrian Rogers of Love Worth Finding Ministries. In it Rogers stated, "You say, 'Well, I give God a place in my life.' God doesn't want a place in your life. Then you say, 'Well, I give God prominence in my life.' God despises prominence in your life. God demands *preeminence* in your life. He will take nothing less. Is there anyone or anything in your life that takes precedence over God? Confess it and repent of it. Now, put on the throne the rightful Master—the Lord Jesus!"

Embracing an idol is always a royal loss.

Seven years ago I quit celebrating my birthday. Because getting older didn't sound like fun to me, I established an annual "Queen Day" instead. Old friends, new friends, and my family have embraced Queen Day and my self-appointed title of "The Queen." I've received lots of queen stuff to commemorate my special day—socks, cards, scepters, pins, pillows, and pictures—but I hadn't laughed as hard about my special day until my friend Josh tickled me royally pink.

I spent an afternoon at Barnes and Noble working away on this book. I stopped by the ladies' room, where I placed my library book and cell phone on top of the bathroom tissue dispenser in the stall. I stood and turned to flush—and in one motion swept my cell phone into the toilet with my sleeve.

"Oh, no! No! No!" Without hesitation, I plunged my hand into the toilet. I was sure my phone was done for, but I miraculously recovered it. I dried it as best I could with paper towels, then raced home and used my blow dryer to evaporate any lingering drops of water.

That night after I reported the mishap to Josh, he sent me an e-mail to comfort me by letting me know that I'm unusually talented, one of a small percentage of people in the world who could do something so graceful. Then he added, "Given your queen status and your mishap with the cell phone, I have one question: Was it a 'royal flush'?"

Thankfully, my "royal flush" didn't turn out to be a royal loss, because my phone was spared. But there are things in life that *are* royal losses—such as trading God for an idol.

Idols leave you feeling empty.

If you and I could sit down over a cup of coffee and I asked you, "How would you describe an idol or a lesser love?" you might say it's a lie, a false god, a seduction, or a deception. But would you describe it as *emptiness*? According to my *New Testament Word Study Bible*, the word "idol" means this very thing. I find this definition interesting, because we don't usually believe our idols are emptiness. Otherwise we wouldn't cling to them. Instead, we believe they're *something-ness*. We may even think, *Sure, my idol doesn't really satisfy me, but at least it has some value.*

God has a different idea.

If something is empty, it's empty. It's not partially empty or sort of empty or a little bit empty—it's just empty! This means that idols can't bring lasting peace or satisfaction to anyone's life, so allowing anything or anyone but God to top your list of dreams, hopes, or desires is a waste of time and life. When we think that we can run from God and embrace idols to find love, satisfaction, peace, or any kind of lasting fulfillment, we're only fooling ourselves. This is the first reason that idols are a royal loss.

Maybe you're thinking, *Wait a minute! How can this be? My idol is desirable. It makes me feel good, so how can it be bad? I can't believe it's empty!*

Granted, at first, idols may give the impression that they'll satisfy. But they never deliver. Idols lure us in with great promise, but once we embrace them, they mock us.

In his book *The Healing Path,* Dan Allender writes that the goal of evil is to "offer glory, then give nothing but heartache, impotence and shame."

In C. S. Lewis's book *The Screwtape Letters,* Screwtape, a worldly wise old devil, echoes Allender's statement when he coaches his nephew, Wormwood, a novice demon, on how to seduce someone. "To get the man's soul and give him nothing in return—that is what really gladdens Our Father's [Satan's] heart."

This is the danger of idols: they never deliver the satisfaction we desire. They lie. They're empty. They lead to royal loss. Remember: they have power over us only if we believe they'll give us something we want. That's what happened to Trina.

Trina was a plain, quiet, and insecure teen who felt insignificant. She longed to be accepted by her peers, but she felt uncomfortable making friends. She spent most weekends alone. When she worked at a donut shop and gained forty pounds during her senior year of high school, she felt even more unimportant. Over the years, she prayed that God would provide the acceptance she longed for through friends or romance, but it never happened.

When she married, she had some hope that she would be accepted and loved the way she had always desired. Instead, after ten years of marriage, her handsome husband had an affair with a beautiful twenty-something woman. Why had God not given Trina the acceptance she desperately wanted and needed? Trina felt betrayed by God and her husband.

Trina's desire for acceptance turned into a desperate, demanding obsession. She *had to* find the significance that she craved, no matter the cost. Acceptance became Trina's idol of the heart (Ezekiel 14:3). When she didn't get acceptance, she began living like a spiritual orphan. She thought, *Okay, God—you didn't give me what I wanted when you knew I needed it, so I'm going to do it my own way. I'm going to get my needs met one way or another!*

Trina turned to beauty to garner the acceptance she craved. She developed a self-improvement plan based on a popular television makeover show. When mothers in her MOPS (Mothers of Preschoolers) group praised her for losing weight, her hopes soared. She traded in her T-shirts and leggings for tight jeans and low-cut blouses. She wore high heels instead of her usual tennis shoes; she became a blond—because blondes have more fun, right?

With every improvement of her appearance, Trina became more internally conflicted. On one hand, she liked what she had become; on the other, she hated it. She hated that she had betrayed herself by becoming artificial. She hated that she felt as if men wanted her only for sex. She despised that no amount of makeup, exercise, or weight loss could bring her the genuine acceptance she craved, and she loathed the fact that she still felt dissatisfied. Nonetheless, she still believed that if she tried a little harder she would finally get what she wanted.

Trina took Botox treatments, had plastic surgery, and purchased numerous age-defying products. Her friends nicknamed her Barbie, and her husband praised her. But when she realized that her beauty couldn't silence her inner turmoil, she had an affair and divorced her husband. Ultimately, Trina never found peace.

What if Trina's desire for acceptance hadn't been her idol? What if her desire for physical beauty hadn't trumped God? What if Jesus had become her all? What if she hadn't felt betrayed by God?

Anything we want too much has the potential of threatening our relationship with God. Through our desperate, demanding desires, Satan can lead us to messy places where idols deceive us. There's nothing wrong with God-given dreams, hopes, and desires, but when they aren't submitted to Christ, when our relationship with Him doesn't top our list of desires, it can lead to personal devastation. Any affection can become an idol that rules us if we allow it a place of prominence in our lives.

We can't fully embrace God and an idol at the same time.

In the 1950s, when dating a girl more than three times didn't mean you were an item, my friend Jim romanced three women simultaneously. He was apparently a glutton for punishment.

Although Jim was able to juggle three women at once, have you ever tried romancing God and an idol at the same time? It's impossible. In Jeremiah 2:11 we're cautioned that when we embrace an idol there is always an "exchange" that takes place. We trade full relationship with God, our glory, for a little god that's not a god at all, for something worthless and empty.

In describing Judah's departure from God to chase idols, God says, "Be appalled at this, O heavens, and shudder with great horror" (Jeremiah 2:12).

Can you imagine the heavens, all the angels, God, and Jesus shuddering at this exchange of glory for emptiness? Can you imagine all of heaven gasping, "Oh, no! How awful! Look at what's happening! They're trading God for *that*? For that little, worthless, nothingness of a god?"

When we exchange God for an idol, it's an exchange that horrifies the heavens. There is no way to fully love God and embrace an idol simultaneously. It's impossible. This is the second reason idols are a royal loss.

The good news is that if you've traded God for a lesser love because you've felt betrayed by Him—or for any reason—He'll take you back.

God is saying, "Return to me."

When I came to Christ, no one warned me that other loves would tug on my heart during seasons of disappointment. I had no idea that my reaction to an unfulfilled desire could threaten my love relationship with Christ. I also didn't expect I would sometimes feel like straying from the God who is worthy of all my praise.

And I didn't anticipate that God would relentlessly chase me—in spite of my wanderings.

His persistent pursuit has amazed me and sometimes brought me to tears. In the Bible, this same passion for me—and you—is represented in His relationship with Israel, an adulterous nation who all too often served other gods and practiced pagan religions. As I've sometimes been, Israel was unfaithful to a love that would never let her go.

But God still pursued.

The third chapter of Jeremiah is a beautiful picture of this pursuing love. Four times in fifteen verses, God says, "return to me," after His people have wandered and "committed adultery" with idols (verse 9). Only a man who truly loves his wife asks her to come back after she has repeatedly cheated on him. This is the kind of love God has for me. *It's the kind of love He has for you.*

When we allow idols first place in our hearts, God says, "Return to me." Heaven holds its breath as He waits for our return. All that's required is the sincere desire to renew our relationship with Him.

Examine Your Heart

1. In this chapter what made the biggest impact on you?

2. Have you ever wanted something or someone so badly that you were willing to trade in relationship with God—permanently or momentarily—to get it? If yes, what was the result? Have you spoken with God about this and received His forgiveness?

3. What things in your life do you want most? Could any of these things come between you and Christ during a time of disappointment if you don't get them?

4. Is there something you want so much that it currently trumps your relationship with God? If yes, why?

5. In this chapter it is stated that idols are empty and that we sometimes seek them because we feel empty. Can you think of a time you chased after an idol? Did you feel empty or dissatisfied during that time?

6. How does it make you feel to know that God is saying, "Return to me," if you've embraced an idol and if something or someone has taken priority over Him?

Action Point

In this chapter a short quiz is included to determine if you've allowed someone or something you desire to become an idol. If you haven't taken the quiz, take it now and talk with God about it. Be honest. Don't allow guilt to get the best of you. Instead, know that He accepts you as you are but wants to help you find satisfaction in Him. Take time to allow the Holy Spirit to speak to you.

6
Feeling Betrayed by God Leads to Sin

Satan . . . sets before us such objects of temptation that are most agreeable to our natures.
—Charles Spurgeon, *Spurgeon on Prayer and Spiritual Warfare*

The betrayed often becomes the betrayer.
—Dan B. Allender, *The Healing Path*

I was browsing the Internet one afternoon when I came across <www.exchristian.org>, a web site with hundreds of posts by people proudly proclaiming that they no longer believe in Christ or Christianity. Some of them have turned to atheism and cults, some to witchcraft and Satanism, and many of them say they've found freedom in their new "enlightenment." As I read their stories, I wanted to lift my head up to heaven and wail.

One thirty-year-old male describes himself as a "modern Job." When he was a child, a man sexually abused him on a playground. I can't imagine the devastation of such an event. Now this man has sadly walked away from God because he feels betrayed. "There are many, many examples of God's cruelty in the Bible," he writes. "But the Bible always blamed human beings instead of the angry, jealous God who created the situation in the first place." This man now describes himself as a searching apostate.

One young man describes how he walked away from Christ at age eighteen because "My whole life, prophets said that I would be a musician and that God would do great things through me. I'd read things in the Bible where God was supposed to prosper His children. After years of being humble and patient, I'm sick of it. I think I have the right to be a little selfish when these things that I've been promised aren't even close to coming true. I'm in a stagnant music project, and I struggle to pay the bills every month." Because he feels betrayed, is prideful, and believes roots of deception, this young man is now leaning on philosophy for guidance instead of the wisdom and love of Christ.

Another web site visitor became disillusioned when God didn't answer her prayers the way she thought He should: "I believed Christians when they told me God would always help me and care about me. At first I thought prayer really worked. Later I realized that nothing at all had happened; I had only believed

God was real and would help, because I really wanted it to be true." This woman is now investigating Buddhism.

Do you see how each of these people believed roots of deception, felt betrayed by God, and then acted on his or her feelings by deserting Him? When someone turns away from Christ and falls into sin, there's always a clear progression from the *feelings* of betrayal to the *actions* of betrayal.

It's dangerous to hold to the lie that God is a betrayer. If we allow something or someone other than God to become our chief desire, then pride, human reasoning, or emotions begin to rule us. It can take us to desperate places we never intended to go. When this happens, ironically the one who felt betrayed by God betrays Him.

When Nina's fiancé called off the wedding two days before it was to take place, she felt betrayed by God. She reasoned that if God is good, He wouldn't allow so many bad things to happen in the world, and He certainly wouldn't have allowed her heart to be broken. Things went from bad to worse when her fiancé quickly married someone else. Because her fiancé had been blessed with marriage—and she was still alone—she doubted that there was a benefit to serving God. "I don't think He rewards those who love Him," she said.

Because she was angry, disappointed, and felt betrayed by God, Nina took matters into her own hands. *If God isn't going to help me with my personal life, then I'll get what I want myself,* she thought. She quickly entered into a rebound marriage and was divorced three years later when her husband turned out to be abusive.

Candace was an admired pastor's wife and women's leader. Then the unimaginable happened: her husband had an affair, and he and Candace divorced. Every miracle she thought God had done in her marriage seemed like a lie. When Candace believed that God had abandoned her, she felt betrayed. From there, things only got worse when she embraced a promiscuous lifestyle.

Stories of people who feel betrayed by God and as a result fall into sin are not uncommon. We're vulnerable to falling into sin for many reasons, but we're especially vulnerable when we experience a broken heart.

In *The Screwtape Letters*, by C. S. Lewis, Screwtape, a senior demon, writes to his novice-demon nephew Wormwood and coaches him on how to do spiritual battle against humans. "The attack has a much better chance of success when the man's whole inner world is drab and cold and empty."

Have you known someone who believed that God betrayed him or her, and then in the aftermath of heartbreak, when the person's inner world was drab, cold, empty, and in a shambles, did something self-destructive? Can you relate? I certainly can.

Believing God is a betrayer is like leaving the window open for Satan to get in.

Yvette Maher, the friend whose story I told in the first chapter, often tells her children that if they allow nefarious things to come into their lives, it's like leaving a window open for Satan to come through. Premarital sex, listening to ungodly music, or engaging in pornography are open windows for the enemy.

Believing that God is a betrayer is an open window too.

Once a woman believes one or more roots of deception, pinning a perceived injustice on God—scattering seeds of betrayal in her heart—the result is an open window for Satan to reach through to draw her into more sin. This is why we must diligently guard against harboring bad feelings toward God.

It's important to note that not everyone who feels betrayed by God abandons Him and becomes a cultist or a witch or completely walks away from Him. Instead, many fall into subtler sins as a result of feeling betrayed by God even as they still confess love for Him. A woman can unknowingly bury her feelings of betrayal where neither she nor others can detect them. As I did, she can attend church, sing songs, tithe, and participate in every ministry under the sun even though she believes God has let her down. Unfortunately, if she doesn't know or admit that she feels betrayed, it doesn't insulate her from Satan's enticements to sin.

That is how it was with me.

After losing the man I loved, even though I felt betrayed by God, I would have said that I still loved Jesus—and that was true. But because I hadn't worked through my feelings of betrayal and eradicated the roots of deception, I was a sitting duck for Satan's seduction. My feelings of betrayal were his opportunity to entice me.

One day a handsome pilot asked me to have lunch with him. I suspected he didn't share my faith, but I was curious, and besides, he was so handsome. On my way to the restaurant I complained to God, *When is it going to be my turn to get married? Everyone else has someone except me.* My attitude should have been a clue that I was in the danger zone of rebellion.

Over lunch, I discovered that he did not share my convictions—just as I thought. But he was so cute and attentive, and he liked me a lot. Over the next few months, I flirted with sin. Because I believed God had let me down in love during my college years, I didn't feel I could trust Him to meet my relational needs. I could certainly do a better job of running my romantic life than He could!

For a short time, I traded obedience and full relationship with God for the handsome pilot. Thankfully, Jesus snatched me from the fire before I got badly burned. I can only imagine how that story might have ended. Trust me—it never pays to believe that God is a betrayer or to hold a grudge against Him.

Before we go any further, let's take a look at the process of experiencing a broken heart (not getting something on our list or getting something that we didn't want) to falling into a hole of sin. To do so, review the four stages of growth of a betrayal weed, covered in chapter two.

Let's dig a little deeper into step five by defining what "falling into sin" is, how it happens, when we're most vulnerable to it, who Satan can use to help make it happen, and what specific emotions are involved in falling into sin when we feel betrayed.

It's scandalous.

When I was playing high school basketball, "offense" meant that my team had the ball and was heading to the hoop. When I became a young adult, I learned that "offense" meant that someone is angry or his or her feelings are hurt. In scripture, though, "offense" isn't either one of those things. It's the name given for the process of leading someone into sin.

The word "offense" is found fifteen times in the New Testament and twenty-five times in the Old Testament. The Greek word for this term is *skandalon*, which means "trap." Sounds like our English word "scandal," right?

According to <www.m-w.com>, Merriam Webster's on-line dictionary, scandal involves—

- Impropriety
- "Discredit brought upon a religion by a seemingly religious person"
- Disgraces
- "Conduct that causes or encourages a lapse of faith or religious obedience in another," and
- "The loss or damage of reputation."

Based on these definitions, do any of the above stories sound as if they involved scandal? Of course! Nothing good can come from being involved in a scandal, which is exactly what *offense*, or *falling into sin by being trapped and led into sin,* involves. Please note that scandal can involve a lapse of faith. To God, losing faith when we feel betrayed by God is scandalous—not to mention that it breaks His heart.

Offense involves an enticement to sin that leads to ruin.

If you and I could sit together and make a list of all that is involved in a scandal, it would undoubtedly include enticement. The man who becomes involved in a scandalous affair is enticed by a woman; the woman who is involved in a scandalous prostitution ring can be enticed by drugs; the business man who is in involved in a scandalous financial scheme is enticed by greed, money, fear, or a host of other things.

It's the same way when we experience the scandal of offense, or being led into sin. There is always an enticement involved, and that enticement *always* leads to ruin.

I found the following statement in my *New Testament Word Study Bible* about the scandal of offense.

In scripture, offense always denotes the enticement or occasion *leading to conduct which brings with it the ruin of the person (in question.)* In the New Testament, the concept of *skandalon* is concerned mainly with the fact that it *incites certain behavior which leads to ruin* and rarely denotes merely a hidden, unexpected cause of ruin.

Did you catch that? Offense *always* involves an enticement to sin that leads to ruin. So what does that mean for the person who is harboring bad feelings against God and believes that He is a betrayer? That means the person had better be on guard against Satan's enticements! Believing that God is a betrayer makes us easy targets for Satan to entice us into sin.

Do any of the enticements in the following stories sound familiar?

- Julie was miserable. Though she prayed for her marriage to improve, it didn't. When she was convinced God didn't care and had betrayed her, she was enticed by an attractive and charming man and became pregnant.

- Cynthia wanted to be a mother but was unable to conceive. She felt betrayed by God. When she learned that her neighbor had a newborn, she lay in bed and thought about how she could get the child. Eventually she was enticed to steal the infant.

- Becky wanted to be like her sister, because she believed her father loved her sister more. After years of prayer, when her father's heart hadn't changed toward Becky, she felt betrayed by God, her father, and her sister. When a friend told Becky that she had the right to harbor a grudge, she was enticed to cut off ties to all three. Ten years have passed since she has talked to any of them.

- Barb thought wealth could buy her love. Because she didn't trust God to provide for her, she was enticed by Satan's seductive lies about money and trampled one person after another on her way up the corporate ladder. Sadly, at forty-five she died friendless and alone.

- When Christy turned thirty-five, she became fed up that God hadn't given her a mate, so she took matters into her own hands. She was enticed through the suggestion of a neighbor to go to a bar, find a man, and sleep with him. She got a husband all right, but she chose an unfaithful man. Now she wishes she had waited on God.

- Keisha was heartbroken when she was raped by a college boyfriend. When doubts about God's goodness led her to harbor feelings of betrayal against God, she was enticed by

Satan's lies about herself and God to become involved in many promiscuous relationships.

• When Robyn felt trapped in her role as a mother, she cried out to God for help in raising her children. When the problems didn't improve with her kids, she felt that she couldn't take it anymore. Then, when Robyn heard about another woman who left her family, she was enticed to do the same.

These stories show that anything is possible when a person feels betrayed by God. Notice that these enticements to sin came through various sources: others, circumstances, and Satan's suggestions.

An unfulfilled desire plus feelings of betrayal equals fertile ground for an enticement to sin.

Satan won't seduce you with something that you don't want. Instead, he'll entice you with a way either to get what you want—like the woman who stole another woman's baby—or to replace what you wanted if there's no way you can have it—like the woman who married on the rebound after her beloved left her two days before their wedding. When you believe God has betrayed you, Satan is more than happy to provide an alternate way to get what you want, which leads to sin.

An unfulfilled dream, hope, or desire can become dangerous if not surrendered to Christ. If we want something too much, it can become a threat to our relationship with God. Satan can use what we long for most to seduce us into sin. We shouldn't be surprised. After all, when's the last time you were tempted by something you *didn't* desire? Our enemy knows what we want most and is skilled at creating custom temptations to match our deepest longings.

James wrote about this: "Each one is tempted when, by his own evil desire, he is dragged away and enticed. Then, after desire has conceived, it gives birth to sin; and sin, when it is full-grown, gives birth to death" (James 1:14-15).

Maybe you're thinking, *This scripture doesn't apply to my desires, because mine aren't evil. I just want to be loved, accepted, successful, and have meaning in my life. There's nothing wrong with that.*

I agree—there's nothing wrong with God-given desires. But when any longing is not submitted to Christ, it can lead to the devastation James describes. Desperate longings can make us do desperate things. A dream, hope, or desire that's not submitted to Christ can threaten our sensibility, causing us to justify our behavior and make excuses. When we give in to Satan's enticements, it often means we're not trusting God to provide. As a result, we settle for crumbs when God wants to give us an entire cake.

Spend some time with God, confess your unbelief, and let Him comfort your fearful heart. Then take a bold step toward obedience by saying no to Satan's enticements.

It's absolutely necessary to resist believing God is a betrayer in order to enjoy a life of peace and joy.

The ruin of offense can occur any time after heartbreak.

When God began teaching me about offense, I thought that the *ruin*—or the result of offense—always came on the heels of the first *feelings of betrayal,* that it happened right away. Then I learned that as long as a woman harbors bad feelings against God and distrusts Him, it makes her an easy target for the enemy, which means she can be enticed into sin that leads to ruin anytime—two minutes after heartbreak or twenty years later. The situation I described above in my life happened eight long years after I first felt betrayed by God.

The ruin of offense can happen during any season of life.

I met with a friend to discuss this book, specifically the topic of falling into sin as a result of feeling betrayed. "So the book is milk for the new Christian," she said. I later thought about that statement and concluded that she was wrong. Offense and an enticement to sin can happen at any season of life, no matter how spiritually mature we are.

Remember Job? The Bible says that he feared God, shunned evil, and was blameless and upright (Job 1:1). We can safely say that Job recognized his place as a servant. No doubt his faith was mature. But that didn't stop Satan from trying to cause Job to feel betrayed, turn away from God, and curse Him. If maturity level were a factor or age were an issue, Satan wouldn't have tried. Make no bones about it: we can be enticed into sin that leads to ruin, from believing that God has betrayed us, at any stage of faith or season of life.

Note that the ruin of offense that comes through an enticement doesn't happen only when we do something considered self-destructive that we *act out*, as in the above examples, but it can also occur when we're unable to *receive* something good God wants to give us, such as love, a family, a new job, a better place to live, or any other gift. Remember: it's difficult to receive anything from someone you we trust.

Because I thought God couldn't be trusted with my personal life, I shut myself off to romantic love. Mine was a scandal of the heart. Is there anything that you haven't received because you believe that God has betrayed you and can't be trusted?

Before there's an enticement to sin, we'll experience the emotions of offense.

I once visited <www.khouse.org>, the web site of author and Bible scholar Chuck Missler, and discovered that there are also emotions involved in the process of offense or being led into sin. According to Missler, offense involves—

- disapproval, which hinders one from acknowledging His authority;
- distrust and deserting one whom you ought to trust and obey;
- judging someone as unfavorable or unjust.

Don't these feelings of disapproving, distrusting, and judging as unfavorable sound just like what one experiences when she feels betrayed by God? Having these emotions about God can make anyone vulnerable to Satan's enticements, especially when coupled with the actions of deserting God and not acknowledging His authority.

Can you relate to these feelings about God? If so, I invite you to begin a conversation with Him right now, confess your feelings, and ask Him to show you His truth and rebuild relationship with Him so that you can avoid the scandal of offense and Satan's enticements!

When Christian musician Tammy Trent lost her high-school-sweetheart husband in a diving accident in the Blue Lagoon in Jamaica, her heart was crushed. I spoke with her once, and she confessed a time when she was almost enticed into sin because of the normal and very human desire that everyone has to be loved:

I love being in love. I'm passionate. And because of that, my heart can be weak. I wanted to feel loved after losing Trent. There were a few guys I had known for a long time, and I was missing love in my life. A relationship with one of these men began to unfold. This was right at the time I started to travel with the Women of Faith Revolve Tour for young girls. The relationship was unhealthy. This could have been something bad. My assistant saw it and recognized that I was about to get into a mess. She sent me a long e-mail. She said,

"As a friend, let me tell you what I see that you can't see." She was worried that I would be mad, but I thought, *She's right,* and I wanted to be accountable. So I wrote the guy and told him that I couldn't have a relationship with him.

Tammy thwarted Satan's attempts to entice her into a sin that could have led to ruin. She did what God wants all of us to do, and that's to put Christ in first place in our lives.

But what if you didn't do what Tammy did? What if, like those described in this chapter, you have completely turned away from God or have been enticed into another sin that has led to ruin because you felt betrayed?

Take heart—God still loves you.

God matches the scandal of offense with forgiving, gracious love.

Have you ever experienced a night when you just couldn't sleep? Last night was like that for me, because something I read online hit me hard before I hit the pillow. When I should have been getting my beauty sleep, I was thinking about love instead.

Around 9 P.M. I had visited a blog written by a man named Tom who lost his wife to breast cancer. As part of his journey through grief, he's recording his heartache—and his hope.

He's also remembering love. And that's why I woke up groggy this morning.

"My love for her will never fade," he wrote. "[It] was a love of devotion with no conditional boundaries. I would marry her all over again if I knew we had to face the adversity of breast cancer."

Ah! I thought, *What kind of love is that?* His words pierced my heart with longing. Doesn't everyone deeply desire that kind of acceptance, to be valued and cherished without condition, even when we're not our best?

As I woke this morning, my longing for romance was replaced with thoughts of Jesus. I wondered if He would die for me all over again if He knew how difficult I would be—if He knew my stubbornness, pride, and imperfections. Of course, because He does know everything about everyone—and in advance. The answer is obvious: *Yes! He loves me like that!*

And He loves *you* like that.

Even when you're not your best and when you're sick with sin. If He had to—and I'm thankful that He doesn't—He would do it all again. This is love that trades the scandal of offense for forgiving, gracious love.

Dear daughter of God, even if you've been enticed into sin because you believed that God has betrayed you, Jesus longs to show you compassion (Isaiah 30:18). He's holding out forgiveness to you so you can run home to Him and He can heal your heart.

Examine Your Heart

1. Have you been enticed into sin that has been a result of feeling betrayed by God?

2. Why do you think we're more vulnerable to Satan's enticements when we feel betrayed by God?

3. What role do you think not surrendering to God's plans for our lives has in being enticed into sin after feeling betrayed?

4. What do you think it means to be "enticed into sin that leads to ruin"? Are there different kinds of ruin?

5. Do you see anything wrong with the young man's attitude who abandoned relationship with God because he hadn't seen his musical dreams materialize?

Action Point

If you realize that you've been enticed into sin as a result from believing God has betrayed you, find a quiet spot and take out a pen and a pad of paper. Write a love letter to God, and tell Him how you feel. Confess your sin; accept His forgiveness, and write anything else to Him that He puts on your heart.

7
Trying to Make God in Your Image

If I can boss a guy around, what do I need him for?
—Jennifer Sugg

God is not like you.
—Eric Stillman

I once went to Wyoming with a former roommate to visit her fiancé, whom I had never met. Before we arrived, she warned me: "He lives in a total bachelor pad. You'll see. He has a sign hanging over his front door that says, 'Dust is holding this house together.' He has an extensive collection of Star Wars characters and two large golden labs."

When we arrived, I handled everything well: the dust, the large collection of characters from Happy Meals, and the dog hair. I even did well with the stuffed, dead animals hanging on the walls. But I have to admit that I went to bed that night and reflected on how it often seems as if men are from another planet. *How in the world do women ever connect with them?*

The truth is that sometimes they don't. But in an effort to connect, and sometimes in an effort to be bossy, a woman tries to mold her man into what she believes he should be, because she's convinced that she can help him improve. She'll tell him how he should dress and comb his hair, what kind of food he should eat, who he should hang out with, and how he should drive. She tells him that he should be more communicative, more tender, more adventurous, more organized, more financially stable, more this, more that.

I once read a short reflection by the late Ruth Bell Graham, wife of Billy Graham, confessing that she had treated her husband this way. Ruth said that her marriage to Billy improved when she realized it was not her job to change him, but God's. In admitting she wanted to change Billy, she admitted that she had an idea of who he should be to be an acceptable husband. This reminds me of how we can sometimes be with God. We have ideas of how He should act to be an acceptable God, especially when we're desperate for something or someone we desire.

Like a bossy bride, we tell Him how and when He should answer our prayers, because we know what's right for us; how He should manifest His power in the world, because we know what's fair; and how He should treat our friends, because we know what's good. Caution: making God in your own image can lead to believing that God is a betrayer when life doesn't turn out the way we wanted.

We can become especially bossy when we're terrified that what we want to happen won't and that what we don't want to happen may—and we're convinced that we won't be able to live with anything less than what we desire. We start thinking that maybe if we can box God in, we can make Him behave.

Trying to make God in our own image is like trying to tell Him how to drive.

When I was a junior in high school, my cousin Barbi and I drove home together following cheerleading practice. One day as I rambled along a country road toward her home, Barbi spontaneously and enthusiastically shouted, "Hey! Let's trade places!" When she started climbing on my shoulders as if we were doing a cheerleading stunt, I knew that she had no intention of waiting for me to stop the car before she pushed me out of the driver's seat.

Why did she want to do something so dangerous? I don't know, but a while back I learned from a counselor friend that the frontal lobe of the human brain that controls reasoning and long-term consequences isn't fully developed until we hit the age of twenty. *That explains it. She had part of her brain missing. Poor thing.*

"Get off me!" I shouted. She persisted. Because she was blocking my view, I foolishly surrendered to her demand. Within seconds the car slid into the ditch, where we stayed until someone came and pulled us out.

When a woman makes God in her own image, it's as if she's trying to push Him out of the driver's seat of her life; she's trying to force Him to do things her way because she's convinced she can arrange her life better than the Lord Almighty. Imagine that!

God addresses this problem when He says, "You turn things upside down, as if the potter were thought to be like the clay!" (Isaiah 29:16). In short, God is saying, "You've got it backwards. You're trying to be the one in charge as if you're driving your own life, but you're not. I am."

Are you tired of bossing God around and trying to make Him in your own image? Let's identify three ways we try to take the wheel from God.

Three Ways We Try to Take Over for God

Prayer

Prayers are of many different types. Some are lifted to God through tears, shouts, or whispers. Some are canned, and we know them by heart. We read others off the back of a book, the back of a bus, or the back of someone's T-shirt. We shoot some up to heaven in the grocery store checkout line, in the shower, or when we're stuck in traffic.

I used to think that all prayers made to the God of the Bible were good. But that isn't true, because not all prayers come from pure hearts that desire for God's will to be done on earth "as it is in heaven."

Instead, some prayers are attempts to boss God around. Prayer can be a way of making God in our own image, of trying to push Him out of the driver's seat.

Crazy! Humans—the grasshoppers of the earth (Isaiah 40:22)—telling the God of the universe what to do. Some people even have the notion that the phrase "in Jesus' name" is some kind of magic statement guaranteeing a favorable answer from the Father.

But it isn't that at all.

Imagine living in a country where a king reigned, and I came to you and said, "In the name of the king I command you to bow to me." What would you do? Of course, you would bow, because I would be representing the king; I would be coming "in his name." This is what it means to pray in Jesus' name: It means to represent Christ and His will in prayer, which means we stand for what He stands for, and we reject what He rejects. It doesn't mean we're toting a magic potion in a three-word sentence to get what we want at the expense of discipleship, obedience, and surrender to God's rule.

Sadly, if we demand that Christ answer our petitions because we've prayed "in Jesus' name" or because we've commanded this or that "in Jesus' name," it can lead to accepting the lie that God is a betrayer or that He's unfaithful when the answer we want doesn't fall into our laps. In all issues of life, it's critical to let God be God.

In the blog "Higher Things Daily Reflections," published by Higher Things, a Lutheran youth organization, John Rosendahl writes, "Sadly, this notion of manipulating God through prayer is a very popular one today. Christians send out prayer-chain letters or e-mails, wrongly assuming that if enough folks are praying, they can move God to respond. They treat the Lord like a divine vending machine, depositing just the right amount of prayers to get their desired result."

Don't get me wrong—prayer can change anything, and the Bible says that we should pray with all kinds of prayers and requests (Ephesians 6:18), but God knows the difference between being used and bossed around and a humble petition. If you aren't sure what your motive is, ask God to show you.

Remember: any doctrine that promises a pain-free life if only we believe enough, do enough good works, or pray hard enough is a setting us up for a nasty fall into a pit of betrayal. Jesus clearly states that "He . . . sends rain on the righteous and the unrighteous" (Matthew 5:45) and "In this world you will have trouble. But take heart! I have overcome the world!" (John 16:33). To deny that trouble touches everyone is to deny the existence of sin.

In his book *What Bothers Me About Christianity,* Ed Gungor writes,

> When I was younger, I used to believe that if a person had enough faith in God, he or she could stop evil. I was a cocky, know-it-all "victory" preacher, and I had faith down to a science. If you prayed the right way, if you believed the right way, if you came to the right church (the one I pastored), you were sure to live a life untouched by evil. And if evil showed up, you just needed to pray harder and immerse yourself more deeply in Bible study. . . . It didn't take long for me to discover that faith and prayer didn't always work the way I thought they were supposed to. Faith was not an exact science.

In his book *When God Doesn't Make Sense,* James Dobson writes that when life hurts and, like Gungor, we embrace a "life-should-always-be-free-from-pain" theology, someone has to take the blame—either us or God—and we typically "stumble toward one of several conclusions: (1) God is dead, irrelevant, bored, or uninvolved in the affairs of man; (2) God is angry at me for some sin I've committed; (3) God is whimsical, untrustworthy, unfair, or sinister; or (4) God ignored me because I didn't pray enough or display enough faith."

All these conclusions create a crisis of faith that makes us believe that God can't be trusted and that He's not loving. What a painful place to be!

When I believed God had betrayed me, I thought if I prayed hard enough and had enough faith, He would give me the answers I wanted. Sadly, I bought into the subtle and deceptive teaching that was my way of trying to be my own god, take the wheel from

Christ, and make Him in my own image. Unfortunately, I was missing out on one of the most important aspects of relationship with God—He loves me with agape love.

John 3:16 says, "God so loved the world that he gave his one and only Son, that whoever believes in him shall not perish but have eternal life." As you may know, the word "loved" in this verse is the verb *agapao* in the original Greek text; the noun for this love is the Greek word *agape.*

Agape love is benevolent love that has the loved one's best interest in mind. One amazing thing about agape is that it's not motivated by what the one loved thinks she needs—that's you and me—but by what God knows she needs—that's God. In a nutshell, God loves us according to what He knows is right for us, so when we pray "in Jesus' name," or when we think, *If I only believe enough, God will answer how I want,* God will say no if He knows it will be best for us and is in accordance with His agape love.

Isn't it wonderful that we have a God who loves us so much that He won't be bossed around?

Making Deals with God

I recently spoke with a man who said, "I did everything I could in the twenty-one years I was married, to be a good Christian husband and father. I attended men's Bible studies. I went to church. I learned about parenting. I loved my wife. Then one day out of the blue she came home and told me that she didn't want to be married anymore. I was shocked. I was so angry at God. I had done everything. I had followed all the rules, but it didn't work." Tears filled his eyes. "I'm still there," he said. "I still feel that God betrayed me."

As we talked, I thought about the deals we make with God, that some of them are unspoken. We make them without realizing what we're doing. Then later, like this man, we find out that the deal was one-sided. He may have been unaware of it, but he had made a deal with God: *God, I'll do my part, and you do yours. I'll be a good husband, and in return, you'll give me what I want. You'll spare me from pain.*

There are other times when we know we're striking a deal with God.

- A fourteen-year-old Jewish Ukrainian girl made a deal with God that she would learn all of the mitzvoth (commandments) in thirty days, and in return, during this same time period, He would make her more beautiful. She shut herself up in a room, and after a month she emerged no more beautiful than when she went in.

- A musician almost drowned in the ocean and told God that he would devote his life to spiritual pursuits if God would save him.

- A woman made a deal with God that if He would spare her mother from cancer, she would devote her life to helping others with the same disease.

- A young lady made a deal with God after witnessing the death of a small child that if she ever became a mother, she must not ever hold her dying child in her arms. "I must not be like that mother," she wrote, "because I do not have that strength inside me. I am not made for that."

Whether we knowingly or unknowingly make deals with God, like prayer, making deals can be a way of gaining control to avoid pain. Also, fear and pride are often the main motivators of wheeling and dealing with God. Sure, sometimes we may make a deal in a moment of human desperation, but it's when we insist on holding God to our one-sided deal and demanding our way that feelings of betrayal can set in.

Early in my Christian walk I told God that if I never married, I wanted Him to let me die, because I was sure I couldn't handle being alone. I've since been reminded that only He knows what we can and can't handle; our job is to trust Him no matter what comes. Is it always easy? No. But it's what He asks of us, and it's the only way to peace.

When we make deals with God, obedience seems useless. In Malachi 3:13-14, God reprimands the Israelites and says, "You have said harsh things against me. . . . You have said 'It is futile to serve God. What did we gain by carrying out his requirements and going about like mourners before the Lord Almighty?'" Because their hopes had not been realized, they felt as if serving God was a waste. Have you ever felt this way?

Have you made deals with God that you have demanded He keep?

Quarreling

My friend Tressa humbly admits that she's like most moms who sometimes reach the end of their parenting ropes. When she's desperate for peace and her three children aren't acting like angels, she can become quarrelsome, barking orders at her kids like a drill sergeant.

It can be the same way when we're desperate to get what we want. When we believe that we *must* have something, we can become quarrelsome, too, shouting orders at God: "Give me what I want, and do it now!"

This is exactly what the Israelites did in Exodus 17:2. When they were desperate for water, they became argumentative. Granted, they had been wandering around in the desert, and they were understandably thirsty. But even though they had many miracles behind them—God had already proven His faithfulness to them by feeding them with bread from heaven and leading them across the Red Sea—they still didn't trust Him, so they argued with Moses, the leader God had appointed. "Give us water to drink," they demanded. Moses said, "Why do you quarrel with me and why do you put the LORD to the test?" Yes, they were quarreling with Moses, but they were *ultimately* quarreling with God. They were testing Him and attempting to make Him in their own image, just as a bossy bride tries to make her man obey her.

In this passage the word "quarrel" in the King James Version is "chide," *riv* in the Hebrew language. It means to toss, grapple, wrangle, strive, contend, quarrel, hold a controversy, plead, conduct a legal case, make a charge, be an adversary, complain. Would you agree that "quarreling" (with God) is a very demonstrative verb?

The phrase, "conduct a legal case" grabbed my attention. When we quarrel with God, we place Him on trial, because we believe He's guilty—when actually He's the only one who has the right to place anyone on trial.

Another part of the definition of "quarrel" in my *Old Testament Word Study Bible* struck my funny bone. "*Riv* [quarrel] has the idea of seizing another by the hair." I thought, *If God had hair and we could see in the natural what happens in the spiritual, some of us would be going around with huge clumps of God's hair in each fist!* I'm sure that if we could pull God's hair, we would.

Have you quarreled with God lately and demanded that He give you something you dream of or hope for? Or have you tried to make Him in your image through prayer or by making a deal with Him? And have you felt betrayed because He hasn't given you what you want?

There are at least three benefits to letting God be God, even when you don't understand what He's doing.

Rest. One of my friends called me recently to discuss a big decision she and her husband needed to make. She laid out the pros and cons, telling me about her concerns and what she thought should happen. She also asked for prayer. I suggested that she let her husband make this important decision.

"Right," she said. "That's exactly it—I want you to pray that God will help my husband make the right choice."

When I hung up the phone, I reflected on the blessed gift of rest that women receive when they let their man "drive." When other women are fretting and having anxiety attacks because they want to make sure everything's perfect, the woman who trusts her man can rest, because she knows he has everything under control.

In the same way, when you let God drive because you choose to trust Him, even when you fear not getting something just the way you want it, a natural rest will occur. Imagine a woman who's trying to wrestle the driver's wheel away from her husband.

Now imagine a woman who's sitting in the passenger seat, allowing her husband to drive without complaining or correcting. Which one do you think is experiencing rest? The one who trusts and is sitting in the passenger's seat, of course. She's enjoying the scenery. She's not fretting about how her husband will get her where she needs to go. She's just relaxing and resting while enjoying her frozen mocha.

The other woman doesn't have time to enjoy a thing, because she's too busy being in control. If she would choose to trust, she could rest too.

Which woman are you?

Jesus says, "Come to me, all you who are weary and burdened, and I will give you rest" (Matthew 11:28). But if you're trying to boss Him around and make Him in your own image, you'll be too busy giving Him orders to give Him your burdens. Therefore, you'll forfeit the rest He promises.

Peace. Psalm 46:10 says, "Be still, and know that I am God." Trying to be in control and relinquish control at the same time just won't work; they can't coexist inside the same heart. When we let God drive our lives and trust that He knows best, we're able to rest and cease from striving, which means that we'll ultimately experience peace.

In the original Hebrew language the phrase "cease striving" indicates giving up by letting our hands down. Isn't that interesting? This means that you can't hold tightly to the steering wheel if you want to experience the peace that comes from letting God drive. Nope, you've got to let your hands down—let go of the wheel. This doesn't mean you sit back and develop a fatalistic attitude about life, however. Instead, you're a co-laborer with God (see 1 Corinthians 3:9), but it also means that you defer to Him when He says no or wait.

Greater communication with God. Have you noticed that it's difficult to effectively and honestly communicate with someone you don't trust or believe has betrayed you? When you're trying to make God in your own image and take the wheel from Him, it's guaranteed that you won't be talking to Him the way you would if you were letting Him drive.

Again, imagine the woman who's trying to steal the wheel from her mate. Imagine what she's saying. The words coming out of her mouth aren't nice, are they? They aren't edifying. They're just plain mean. She's loud. She's obnoxious. She's bossy, and she lacks the self-control the Bible lists as one of the fruits of the Holy Spirit (Galatians 5:22).

Now imagine a woman who's resting in the passenger's seat. It's as though she has honey under her tongue; her words are sweet. Because she's relaxed and doesn't feel threatened, she's kind. She's just chatting away with her man as though it's all blue skies and sun.

When you're trying to steal the wheel from God by making Him in your own image, your communication with Him will be hindered. Or perhaps you'll stop talking to Him altogether.

Words of gratitude will be replaced by complaining, and praise will be ruined by criticism. You'll find that you won't be able to talk with Him with ease, because you'll be thinking that He should be taking you somewhere else. The result of refraining from bossing God around and trying to make Him in your own image will be greater intimacy with Him.

Having the right view of myself in relationship with God (I'm the clay, and He's the potter—Isaiah 29:16) ushers in peace. In the knowledge of my smallness and inadequacy, God's bigness is comforting and empowering. Trying to drive my own life will always drive me right into a spiritual or emotional ditch. There's safety in knowing one's place.

Granted, it's not easy to give in to God and let Him drive, especially when something or someone dear to us is at stake. Surrender is most often a moment-by-moment process. Be encouraged in knowing that if we choose to rest in Him, choose to trust Him, choose to let Him drive, choose to let Him be God, we'll experience greater peace, rest, and communication with the One who loves us enough not to let us always have our way.

Examine Your Heart

1. What part this chapter spoke to you most?

2. Have you ever tried to boss God around through prayer? What was the result?

3. Why do you believe prayer is used as a means to control God—particularly in the United States?

4. Have you ever felt as the Israelites did—that it's useless to serve God? If so, have you made a spoken or unspoken deal with God that He would do what you wanted?

5. If you've made a deal with God, what was your internal motivation? Fear? Pride? Something else?

6. Have you ever quarreled with God to make Him "obey"? If so, what can you do in the future to surrender to Him instead?

7. Which benefit of allowing God to "drive" do you need most in your life right now?

Action Point

Take crayons, markers, or colored pencils, and on a large sheet of paper draw a picture that depicts how you feel when you try to boss God around and make Him in your own image. Then draw how you feel when you let Him have His way. Add scriptures to your composition that support both perspectives. Remember: you're not entering an art contest; this drawing is for your benefit only. It's like journaling with color!

8

Sometimes It Looks as If God Doesn't Care

Maybe it's time to stop putting God in a box the size of your cerebral cortex.
—Mark Batterson, *In a Pit with a Lion on a Snowy Day*

The god an atheist does not believe in is usually not the God of the Bible. Unfortunately the god of the "believer" is also often not the God of the Bible.
—Gerald L. Schroeder, *The Science of God*

Sometimes someone will say something to us, or we'll read something in a book, or a character in a movie will deliver a line that haunts us as we think about where our lives are taking us, where we've been, if God really has control over our lives, and if He even loves us.

A quote from the movie *Forrest Gump* haunted me for a while. At the end of the movie a feather floats on a light wind, and Forrest, played by Tom Hanks, wistfully says, "I don't know if we each have a destiny or if we're just floatin' around accidental-like on a breeze, but I think it's maybe both."

That line was like a knife plunged into my heart. *Oh, God! Were you truly in control of the things that happened in my past and the choices I made? Or was I just like a feather, floating without guidance, without help from you?*

I reasoned that if the decisions I made about my personal life were wrong, even though I had prayed incessantly to God for help in making them, then I had to conclude that He was not in control because He was powerless or passive. It also meant that He had abandoned me, which meant that His love for me was a lie.

For years, questions I never dared utter about God's love and power tormented me. My problem was that I had put God into a box, as Mark Batterson says, the "size of [my] cerebral cortex"—a place far too small for the Almighty.

Doubting God's love and power is not unique. Many of us go through difficult times dealing with the loss of something or someone we hoped for and dreamed of.

God, are you in control? Do you love me?

How we answer those two questions is critical, because without full confidence in God's love and power, trust cannot thrive; and where trust cannot thrive, deciding God is a betrayer is not far behind. After all, what kind of woman can trust a God she believes can't, won't, or doesn't care?

A woman's beliefs about God's love and power are the windows she looks through to view her circumstances. For this reason, believing the wrong things can cause feelings of betrayal when she doesn't get what she longed for or she gets something she didn't want.

These windows of God's love and power are defined by circumstances, church leaders, parents, media messages, society, neighbors, friends, religion, broken promises, Satan's lies, bad theology, and by people who abuse us, reject us and break our hearts, and by our prayers that don't produce the results we were counting on. Our windows of God's love and power are defined from childhood and are continually redefined throughout life, much in the same way our lists of things we dream of, hope for, and desire change over time.

Let's investigate three views—or windows—of God's love and power that can cause a woman to feel betrayed.

Unloving (Harsh) and Powerful God

When I was in elementary school, a junior-high bully followed me across the schoolyard and repeatedly kicked me in the back as I walked home. The God in the first window is a celestial bully. He's harsh and unloving and enjoys watching people suffer. He expects perfection and doesn't give an inch of grace. If you're going to get love from Him, it's because you earned it. You've got to do it right, all the time, and if you don't, you'll pay.

One woman I know struggles with this view of God's love and power. Due to growing up with an abusive and highly critical father, she struggles with being too hard on herself, and she believes the only way to get God to love her is to perform perfectly. Her entire life is affected by this false view—every relationship she engages in and every major decision she makes. She constantly lives in fear of God's retribution and believes He's out to punish her when she sins or makes a mistake.

Are you afraid of God? Do you believe what you do is never enough and that *you* are never enough? If so, consider that fear and love cannot coexist; one always negates the other. First John 4:18 says, "Perfect love drives out fear, because fear has to do with punishment." This truth is powerful because accepting, believing in, and relying on God's love is the secret to overcoming fear.

I recently received an e-mail from a good friend who reminded me, once more, that God is good, not a punishing, mean, angry God to be afraid of—but one who has my best interest in mind:

Each time the suspicion arises that God is really out to get us, bent on making us miserable, or thwarting any good we might seek, we're calling Him a liar. His secret purpose has been revealed to us, and it's to bring us not to ruin but to glory. That is precisely what the Bible tells us about: "God's secret wisdom, a wisdom that has been hidden and that God destined for our glory" (1 Corinthians 2:7).

I know of no more steadying hope on which to focus my mind when circumstances tempt me to wonder why God doesn't do something and if He' against me. He' always doing something—the very best thing—we ourselves would certainly choose if we knew the end from the beginning. He's at work to bring us our full glory.

Here are a few scriptures that show us that God is not out to hurt us, ruin us, or punish us but to promote us:

- Psalm 51:1 says that God's love is unfailing, that He has great compassion, and that He's forgiving.
- Psalm 144:2 says that God is a shield and a refuge.
- Psalm 25:7 says that God is good.
- Psalm 73:26 says that God gives strength to those He loves.
- Psalm 103:8 says that the Lord is gracious.
- 1 Peter 5:6-11 says that God cares for you.

- Psalm 145:8 says that the Lord is gracious and compassionate, slow to anger and rich in love.

Unloving (Passive) but Powerful God

The second window describes a passive father who leaves you to figure out your own problems, even though he could do something about them. This leaves a woman believing she has no value, that she's unimportant.

This is a lie the enemy still uses against me in difficult circumstances, and it's where I camped out most of the time in my life as a new Christian. Because I didn't trust myself to make sound decisions, *and* I didn't believe God would help me, this view left me without an inch of solid emotional or spiritual ground to stand on.

The following scriptures prove that God cannot be a passive father.

- Proverbs 16:9 says we make plans but that God directs our steps.
- Philippians 1:6 says that God will perfect the work He began in us until the day of Christ Jesus.
- Romans 8:28 says that God works all things together for the good of those who love Him.
- Psalm 139 says that God knows when we sit, rise, and speak, and He has known about every day of our lives before one of them came to be!
- Psalm 33:13-15 says that God looks down on all humanity, watches all who live on the earth, and considers everything they do.

Loving (Compassionate) but Powerless God

When I was in sixth grade, I loved serving crosswalk duty after school. While my crosswalk partner and I were as helpful as we could be, we didn't have a lick of power. If a car accident happened, we couldn't give a ticket. If people jaywalked, we couldn't fine them. If someone fell and needed CPR, we were powerless. We had the title, the badge, and we sure were nice, but we didn't have any real power.

The depiction of God in the third window reminds me of a crosswalk guard. He's compassionate and has good intentions toward those He loves, but He can't do anything for them because He's powerless. He would love to help, but He's just too weak. This view of God leaves a woman feeling as if she has to bear the burden of life all alone.

When I recently spoke with my friend over a cup of my favorite tea, we discussed these windows of God's love and power, and Dave described why he believes he struggles with seeing God as a wimpy crosswalk guard.

My mother died when I was nine, and our family was torn apart. My father, although loving and compassionate, felt incapable of raising two boys alone, so he sent my brother and me to live at our aunt's house. I had fun with my cousins, but I felt abandoned by my dad. Now, when I face a problem that needs supernatural intervention, I often believe that God wants to do something about it, but He just can't.

It's interesting that Dave's view of God is that He's like his earthly father was—loving and compassionate but weak and incapable of fixing problems or handling life.

Here are some scriptures that show us why this is a faulty view of God.

- Isaiah 59:1 says that "the arm of the LORD is not too short to save, nor his ear too dull to hear."
- Daniel 4:35 says that God "does as He pleases with the powers of heaven and the peoples of the earth."

- John 19:11 says that those who crucified and tortured Jesus would not have had any power over Him if it had been given to them from God.
- Job 42:2 says that God can do all things and that no plan of His can be thwarted.

In addition to these scriptures, many others support the fact that God does what He wants when He wants and that nothing can stop Him. When you mix that kind of power with the powerful love of God, you know you have a larger-than-life Father on your side who can be trusted.

Loving and Powerful God—the God of the Bible

Some people shout when they get excited; some cry. Lori's hair danced. When I taught middle school in Texas, Lori was one of my special education students. When she was thrilled about something, her brown, curly hair shook, jived, and jiggled like something out of a 1970s disco.

One afternoon Lori rushed toward me with her hair dancing and thrust a piece of paper into my hand. "Look, Miss Schutte! I drew a picture of the devil!"

I didn't know what to say. In an attempt to put a positive spin on a negative topic, I mustered a smile and exclaimed, "Wow! Why don't you draw a picture of God?"

Lori's blue eyes grew dark, and she scowled. Her eyebrows pushed together in the middle of her forehead as if they had been bobby pinned there. She shuffled her feet, looked at the ground, and finally lifted her eyes to meet mine. "Well—well—*no*; I can't draw *that* good," she said.

How profound! How moving! How true!

This is the God of window number four. He can't be "drawn" because He can't be comprehended. He's that magnificent! And for this reason He must be taken on faith rather than on feelings or intellect. He can't be put in a box. To attempt to wrap our minds around Him means that we reduce Him to something that He is not. This God is trustworthy, loves you madly, and is filled with grace and mercy. He's the God who says, "Give me your burdens—I'll help you," "Give me your heartache—I'll heal you," "Give me your life—I'll save you." The God of this window hasn't promised that life will be without problems, but He has promised that when you walk through the fire, He'll be with you. His love is indefinable. His power is perfect.

Not everyone sees God this way. In a survey conducted by the Barna Group, 1,871 self-described Christians were asked questions about God, Jesus Christ, the Holy Spirit, and demons. What they discovered is that not everyone who calls themselves Christians believes in Lori's God.

Seventy-eight percent of those responding to a survey said that God is the "all-powerful, all-knowing Creator of the universe who rules the world today." The remainder chose other descriptions of God that are not consistent with biblical teaching. For example: "Everyone is a god," "'God' refers to the realization of human potential," and so on.

Additionally, Barna reported that "most Christians do not believe that the Holy Spirit is a living force." No wonder we have problems viewing God through the wrong windows, resulting in feelings of betrayal when life is tough.

Can you see how looking through the first three windows could lead us to feel betrayed when life hurts? When looking through those windows, God does not appear to be reliable or trustworthy. But the God of the Bible *is* trustworthy.

God is not always *obviously* loving and powerful, right? He doesn't shout from heaven, send letters to large newspapers, or broadcast His mind over the Internet. I recently spoke with a friend who, like many people, has a problem with this: "Why doesn't He come down and make himself obvious?"

I can think of two answers to my friend's question: (1) God *did* come down and make himself obvious when He came to earth as Christ, and (2) Sometimes God is hidden; sometimes He's hard to find—and He likes it that way, because it presses the issue of faith.

In *The Case for Faith* journalist Lee Strobel interviews Peter Kreeft, a world-class philosopher, who makes the following statement: "The Bible says, 'Seek and you shall find.' It doesn't say that everybody will find him; it doesn't say nobody will find him. *Some* will find him. Who? Those who seek. Those whose hearts are set on finding him and who follow the clues."

In my experience, the greatest clues I've received about God's love and power made personal in my life have not been made most evident through signs and wonders but rather as I've sat alone with Him and listened for His "still, small voice." In this way, He has invaded my reality with a higher reality, one I can't ignore.

I recently spoke with a young man on the patio at a Starbucks near my home who said, "I just can't get connected to God. I'm the kind of person who has to see it and touch it to believe it."

I motioned to the majestic Rockies to the left of where we sat and said, "Steve! Open your eyes! Take a look at those awesome mountains. Think about the wonder of a baby, the beauty and intricacy of a flower, the complexity of a single cell. All of creation is shouting at you that God exists. You *can* see it and touch it!"

Not only does all of creation scream at us that God exists (Romans 1:20), but it also testifies that He's in control of all things. Think about the order of the universe: the sun rises and sets at just the right time; the moon knows its place in the sky; the seasons are ordered and exact.

In the Book of Job God states His control over all creation, including the sea, waves, morning, snow, recesses of the deep, "abode of light", darkness, lightning, rain, water, stars, and constellations. In all this, He says that He has "dominion over the earth" (Job 38:33).

To think that God exercises His authority over lesser things such as snow, stars, and the sea but stops short of involvement in the events of the lives of people doesn't make sense, especially when He has loved us enough to send His only Son to die for our sins (John 3:16).

Can you imagine a man who would die for his daughter as a sin sacrifice but refuse to get involved in the events of her life? Because God loved us enough to send His son to die for us, how much more will He give us all things? (Romans 8:32). He's in control and involved in our lives because His love commands nothing less.

Which of the four views of God most closely resembles your view of Him? Do you feel as if you bounce around to different views? Do you see God as half celestial bully and half passive father, maybe part crosswalk guard and part God of the Bible?

Our views of God's love and power are often inconsistent.

Linda's husband passed away from cancer in January, and she was understandably grieved. Even though she was hurting, she believed that God loves her and that He is powerful enough to carry her through her trial and, when all is said and done, He will be found faithful. The following year she lost the job she loved. Suddenly she finds herself looking through a different window— the one where God seems like a passive father, because He could have done something but didn't. She feels betrayed.

Linda would be wise to ask herself why she has two opposing views of God's love and power. Remember: Scripture tells us that

God does not change. So why do we put God in a box? For instance, why would we believe that He's loving and powerful when it comes to our work lives, but when it comes to our children—even though He's loving—we're afraid He's too weak to protect them? We see Him as a crosswalk guard.

Perhaps we believe that God cares about our friendships but doesn't care about our finances. We're certain He'll bring us through a pregnancy but don't think He's concerned about our preschooler. We think He has the power to heal us from a cold but not from cancer.

You may have complete confidence in God's love and power in many areas of your life, but perhaps there's one area in which you struggle to believe that He's loving and powerful. If that's the case, be on guard! Any area in which you doubt God's love and power is an area Satan can leverage to cause you to believe that He has betrayed you.

To avoid feelings of betrayal, we must walk by faith and not by sight.

The views of God through the first three windows tells us that we're walking by sight, not by faith. That means we're living by what we see in our circumstances rather than the truth.

That is a very dangerous way to live, because Satan will always present us with something in our circumstances that seems to validate the lies—roots of betrayal—that we believe when we're suffering.

In his book *Disappointment with God,* Philip Yancey writes about a friend named Douglas who experienced deep disappointment. Douglas's wife contracted breast cancer. While in the middle of this crisis, a drunk driver swerved across the center line and smashed head-on into Douglas's car, and Douglas received a severe blow to the head. His vision was affected, and his ability to read was hindered. He could hardly walk down a flight of stairs without assistance. The damage was irreparable. Philip interviewed Douglas to ask if he felt disappointment with God. Philip writes,

> Douglas was silent for what seemed like a long time. He stroked his peppery grey beard and gazed off beyond my right shoulder. . . . Finally he said, "To tell you the truth, Philip, I didn't feel any disappointment with God. . . . The reason is this: I learned, first through my wife's illness and then especially through the incident, not to confuse God with life. . . . I have learned to see beyond the physical reality of this world to the spiritual reality. We tend to think, 'Life should be fair because God is fair.' But God is not life. And if I confuse God with the physical reality of life—by expecting constant health, for example—then I set myself up for a crashing disappointment. God's existence, even his love for me, does not depend on my good health. Frankly, I've had more time and opportunity to work on my relationship with God during my impairment than before."

Douglas learned to successfully navigate disappointment when you don't get what you want: to believe without seeing, to walk by faith and not by sight. Douglas knew that God is loving and powerful, even though his circumstances didn't support this truth. Douglas was looking through the right window.

Some people think that trusting God as Douglas did, to believe without seeing, is foolish. "Blind faith," they scoff. But isn't faith most often blind? If faith can see from beginning to end, if faith means that we understand all things like God, then faith is not faith at all.

Walking by faith and not by sight means not living by your emotions.

To walk by faith and not by sight means not giving emotions the freedom to rule our lives. Instead, we let God's truth determine how we respond when life hurts.

This was a difficult concept for me as a young Christian. A sensitive, creative type, I was extremely driven by my emotions. I couldn't grasp how something could be true if it didn't *feel* true. This mind-set made believing God difficult.

Not too long ago I came across a great book that revealed how my emotions led me into a pit of feeling betrayed, even after I became a follower of Christ.

In his book *Roll Away the Stone,* Dutch Sheets shows the difference between our souls—which are made up of mind, will, and emotions and is called the *psuche* in the Greek New Testament—and the spirit (*pnuema*).

Sheets writes, "When you are born again, your spirit is instantly renewed, but it's a different story with the soul."

Our spirits become new creations (2 Corinthians 5:17), and are made complete in Him the minute that we come to Christ (Colossians 2:10). But our souls (mind, will, *and emotions*) can still be tempted by worldly ideas, rebellion against God's truth, and seduction by Satan's lies. Feelings can't be trusted, because they can be very deceptive. A wise woman lives by faith and by what God says, not by what she *feels*. Granted, this doesn't mean that we're unfeeling, but our feelings are governed by truth. Our faith overcomes our feelings.

In his book *The World's Last Night and Other Essays*, C. S. Lewis writes, "Feelings come and go, and when they come, good use can be made of them: they cannot be our regular spiritual diet." Those who let feeling rule the day will, as I did, find themselves in a spiritual ditch.

I recently read a story at <www.exchristian.org> about a young woman who walked away from faith in Christ because she didn't see an instant transformation in her life as she believed should happen based on 2 Corinthians 5:17, which she felt would prove that she was saved. She thought that her mind, will, and emotions should be instantly transformed.

> I've prayed, begged, and done everything I know to do for God to miraculously intervene in all areas of my life, but it seems as though I've been on some sort of self-improvement course relying solely on my strength and resources. Where is God? I'm still sick and bound by some things I can in no way overcome without divine intervention. I had been hoping that by the power of the Holy Spirit I'd be made whole, but I've gone full circle to no avail.

As a result of feeling betrayed by God because she didn't experience immediate transformation, she walked away from God.

It's critical to remember that the transformation of the soul may happen over time as we're exposed to God's truth. This is why it's critical to read the Bible, get to know God's love, listen for His voice, connect to His heart, and read good Christian books. Spending time alone with Christ and accepting His truth are transforming; they're also the antidote for feeling betrayed.

The window you look through determines how you perceive yourself.

Imagine that a little boy named Josh walks to school alone every Friday. With every step that leads him closer to school, Josh's fear builds, because he knows that the minute he moves inside the playground gate, a bully twice his size will be waiting to thump him.

Now imagine that the same little boy walks to school—but instead of walking alone, his big brother, twice the size of the bully, walks behind him. Would Josh be confident? Obviously. After all, his big brother loves him and is powerful enough to protect him. Josh would be freed by the knowledge that someone loving and powerful "had his back." That would make a big difference in the way Josh sees himself.

The window you see God through will determine how you view yourself when you face disappointment.

If you see God as a celestial bully, you'll be fearful; if you see God as a passive father, you'll feel unloved and unimportant. But when you believe that God is loving and powerful, then you'll be able to navigate heartache with greater confidence. That doesn't mean you'll never experience pain, hurt, or disappointment, but you'll know God loves you even in the midst of trouble.

It isn't enough to intellectually accept that God is loving and powerful—you must believe that He's loving and powerful *for you*. Your belief must be personal, not just a corporate ideology that you learned in Sunday School. Theology or religion will never carry anyone through heartache—only having a personal relationship with God and believing wholeheartedly that He is deeply entrenched in your story with love and power will. This is cultivated by knowing Him, spending time with Him, and learning about His heart. Only then can we be saved from believing that God is a betrayer.

Examine Your Heart

1. What in this chapter was most meaningful to you?

2. Which window of God's love and power do you most identify with?

3. Are you experiencing a time of disappointment now? Which window are you looking through? Is this different than the window you were looking through during your last trial? If so, why?

4. How has the window that you've most consistently looked through affected your confidence and view of yourself?

Action Point

Draw the windows of God's love and power on a sheet of paper and label them. Next to each one, write how you've felt about yourself or believe that you would feel about yourself when looking at your circumstances through each window.

9
Heartbreak Creates Questions You Can't Answer

Here are the typical components of a "faith under fire": a very troubling event, an element of injustice or unfairness (why me?), a silent God who could have intervened but didn't, and a million unanswered questions.

—James Dobson, *When God Doesn't Make Sense*

No one can comprehend what goes on under the sun. Despite all his efforts to search it out, man cannot discover its meaning. Even if a wise man claims he knows, he cannot really comprehend it.

—Ecclesiastes 8:17

The secret things belong to the Lord.

—Deuteronomy 29:29

Have you ever been friends with a group of daredevils? I was. While I was a college exchange student at the University of London in the late eighties, I met a young woman named Julie who introduced me to her buddies, a crazy crew who got their thrills from climbing mountains and cliffs.

One weekend Julie and her friends invited me to join them for a camping trip to Cornwall, England, where we slept on a very soggy, sandy, windy beach, shivered in the damp cold, and climbed a cliff near a quaint, tiny town where people talked funny.

Because I like to keep my feet on the ground, I tried to convince my new friends that I couldn't make the climb because I didn't have the right footgear.

"Not a problem!" Julie shouted as she threw a pair of climbing shoes my way. They were just my size. *Oh, brother!* I thought. *Now there's no excuse.*

Reluctantly, I put on my new gear and set out to scale the cliff wall. My confidence grew with every step—until I was only twenty feet from the top.

Then the trouble started.

A large ledge jutted out above me and to my right. And because the cliff wall below was slick, there wasn't anywhere for me to put my feet to gain traction. My only recourse was to shimmy around the ledge using just my not-so-bulging biceps and upper-body strength. In that moment, Spiderman, Batman, Superman, or any man would have been helpful. But it was just me, that menacing ledge, and my oh-so-very-tired arms.

With pride and my aversion to looking like an imbecile in front of my new friends driving me, I attempted the impossible. I started to shimmy around the ledge by holding on with my arms and wiggling my body like a worm hanging from a tree branch, but my attempt didn't last long. Within a minute or two, when I felt as if every ounce of my strength had been zapped from my body, I fell.

Down.

Down.

Down.

And I screamed one very long scream until the rope and climbing harness caught me.

After I had managed to stop hyperventilating, I looked between my dangling legs and realized I was hanging over the Atlantic Ocean. Not knowing whether to laugh or cry, a flurry of questions came to mind: *Now what? How do I get to the top? How far did I fall?* And *Oh, no! What are my friends who witnessed my screaming descent thinking?*

Thankfully, Julie and the others pulled me to the top of the cliff inch by inch and onto solid ground, where I whooped and hollered and made an idiot of myself a second time.

When a woman doesn't get something she wants, or—as in this case—she gets something she didn't ask for, she gets an "I'm-hanging-over-the-Atlantic" experience followed by lots of questions.

We can shout our inquiries to God in a dark night, hold them in our hearts where no one else can see, and wrestle with them until our spirits are exhausted. Sadly, we can also experience the truth that there are few things more painful than a heart that does not trust God and will not allow Him to be in charge of the unknown.

In *When I'm Longing for God*, Paul S. Williams gives insight into our discomfort with unanswered questions:

> In the Age of Science mysteries aren't tolerated at all. They are problems to be solved in the objective environment of the laboratory. "Wonder" itself has been marked for extinction, because there is always a scientific explanation for mystery

and wonder. Anything that can't be logically explained is to be stuffed in a forgotten closet in a seldom-used guest room.

I recently overheard two women talking, and one of them said, "God works in mysterious ways." That's true. But for the most part, we aren't comfortable with the mystery of God. What if we could embrace the unknown of God? What if we could latch onto what He doesn't tell us and find joy in it?

Not only are we uncomfortable with mysteries in general, but we're also uncomfortable with our *personal* unknowns. We want all of our bows tied, our knots untied, and our ducks in a row. We don't like things we can't explain: life situations, relationships, and job losses that fall into the realm of "What happened back there?"

However, if we insist on understanding everything we can't explain, we'll lose heart and courage for the future. To be at peace with life—and especially the things that have broken our hearts—means we give up to the God who does know.

Powerful author and speaker Beth Moore once spoke to a women's group and explained that she finally had the opportunity to confront her sexual abuser. The years of childhood victimization had long since passed, but the memories had not. After she explained to the man how what he did negatively affected her life, she walked away from where she had met him and thought, *He has no idea how what he did affected me.* In that moment, God spoke: I *know.*

It may sound trite, but it's true—God knows, and that's enough. He cares about the questions we can't answer and life's problems that were never resolved.

God uses unanswered questions to build faith.

If you're like I was, you're probably convinced that the only way you'll ever experience peace and happiness is for God to answer all your whys, hows, and what-fors. Maybe you feel His silence signals His betrayal. Remember, though, that God has your best interest at heart. That doesn't mean He'is going to answer every one of your questions; He may not—and for good reason.

Hebrews 11:3 says, "By faith we understand that the universe was formed at God's command." In her Bible study *Living Beyond Yourself* Beth Moore writes,

> What this passage is saying is that there will never be enough conclusive evidence to all humankind that He [God] is the Creator. He has ordained that some questions remain unanswered to force the issue of faith.

In the same way that God will not answer all our questions about His role as Creator so He can force the issue of faith, neither will He answer all our inquiries about personal heartbreak.

If God answered all of our questions, how would our faith be strengthened? There are never enough answers to satisfy a fear-filled heart.

Choosing to trust God in spite of our questions changes us from insecure to secure, from fearful to confident, from ungrateful to grateful. It's *faith* that transforms us into peaceful, confident daughters who are secure in the mighty love of God, even when He's silent.

Maybe you feel that an explanation for your heartbreak trumps the value of faith. I can relate. For many years understanding my heartbreak was more important to me than faith, because I didn't grasp the value of faith. Thankfully, over the years God has shown me that the faith He has produced in me far outweighs the answers He hasn't revealed to me. As it turns out, my faith, and knowing God loves me, has given me all the things I thought having my questions answered would provide me. Now I wouldn't trade my faith for anything—not even for all the answers in the world.

It took time and lots of exposure to the truth of God's Word before I became content to leave the unknown—*unknown*. Through the gift of your unanswered questions, God wants to give you the gift of faith that He says is more precious than gold (1 Peter 1:7).

Questions are like lights on the dashboard of a car.

Think back to the questions you've asked God when your heart has been broken after things didn't turn out as you had planned. Were your questions faith-filled? Did they reveal that you believed God even though you were hurting? Or were they full of doubt about God, yourself, your relationship with Him, or His Word?

Recently a red light appeared on the dashboard of my car. I know almost zero about mechanics, but I do know that when one of those little blinky things comes on, it's "talking" to me about the internal condition of my automobile.

Just as lights on the dashboard of a car reveal what's going on under the hood, the questions we ask during a valley of weeping reveal what's going on in our hearts. If we listen to our inquiries, they'll show us if things are running well with our Savior or if we need a spiritual tune-up.

What's under the hood?

I admire people who trust God even when they experience deep disappointment. My friend Mark is one of those people. Three years after his wife was diagnosed with a rare form of blood cancer, she went home to heaven. It was heartbreaking for Mark to lose the woman he loved after twenty-two years of marriage, but he still chose to trust Christ.

Rather than demand that God tell him why his wife died and left him alone with three sons, he asked questions of surrender:

God, how can I love my boys well through this time of pain? Lord, how can I love others more because of my heartache? Indeed, Mark's questions revealed that under the hood was trust in the God who loves him. The result has been faith that has undoubtedly pleased God (Hebrews 11:6) and peace in the midst of pain.

If any of the following questions of surrender have been a part of your journey with Christ, praise Him for giving you the heart to stay close to Him and obey.

- Lord, what do you want to teach me?
- Jesus, how can I cooperate with you so that my pain will be used for my good and your glory?
- God, how can I grow more in love with you in the middle of this heartache?
- Lord, how can I cooperate with you to prevent Satan from taking advantage of me during this vulnerable time?
- Jesus, how can I glorify you even though I'm disappointed—or hated, or crushed, or in despair?
- My Savior, what can I do to love others more because of what's happening to me?
- God, how can I experience your presence in greater measure during this time of disappointment?
- Jesus, what do you want me to do?

Some questions reveal that there's a lack of trust "under the hood" in our hearts.

While questions of surrender indicate hearts that trust God, some questions reveal a lack of trust. Entertaining questions filled with doubt about God, yourself, your relationship with Him, and His Word is like allowing termites into your mansion of faith. If you let them take over, they'll eventually chew right through your faith foundation, and feelings of betrayal will grow.

Janet experienced this very thing. Like many women, this lovely lady has always wanted to become a mother; it has topped her list of desires. However, a violent rape all but ended her dream. Though she was told by doctors that she couldn't conceive, she has kept hope alive by praying, because prayer can change anything, and God could intervene. But now her biological clock has ticked on, and as the chances of having children have narrowed, her questions for God have multiplied. Unfortunately, Janet put God on trial and declared Him guilty of many things. A large betrayal weed was growing:

- "God, why are you punishing me?"
- "Lord, why do you allow other women to have babies only to dump them in dumpsters—when I would love a child and you won't give me a baby?"
- "God, if you aren't going to give me a child, why don't you take away my desire for a child?"
- "Lord, what did I do wrong? Why are you treating me so badly?"

My heart goes out to this woman because she doesn't believe God's love or sovereignty, and I know firsthand that it's very painful. I wish I could speak with her to tell her that God never allows any pain in our lives that He can't redeem, that He'll bring good from her heartache (Romans 8:28), and that we don't have the capacity to understand the mind of God.

There are as many questions like Janet's as there are circumstances that produce them. Following are some more examples. If you've asked some of these questions, bow your heart to God and tell Him that you want to trust Him no matter how your circumstances look and that you want to have a heart that will let him have His good way in your life.

- "God, why me?"
- "Lord, why do you hate me?"

- "God, why do others have it better than me?"
- "God, why did you give my friend what she wanted, but I've served you and haven't been blessed?"
- "God, can you really do what you say you can?"
- "God, where are you?"
- "Jesus, why have you lied to me?"
- "Lord, why have you told me that you care about me but you don't show it?"
- "Lord, you say in your Word that you give those who love you the desires of their hearts; why isn't this true in my life?"
- "God, I've prayed and prayed for you to change things, but you haven't. Why?"
- "God, why don't you love me?"

I want to make the point that God is not opposed to questions, but He *is* opposed to rebellion. Most of us ask questions—sometimes out of unbelief—in times of heartbreak.

The psalmists asked all kinds of questions when they were hurting, but their questions, even those filled with doubt, always led them back to faith. This is how God wants it to be with you. If your questions lead you away from Him, it's time to reevaluate what you believe about God, yourself, your relationship with Him, and His Word. Remember: the Bible says that "God opposes the proud but gives grace to the humble" (James 4:6).

I've shouted, screamed, cried, and whispered many of the questions listed here. Sadly, I didn't understand how detrimental these inquiries could be. Besides being one of the reasons we can be enticed into sin, which leads to ruin, questions like these can steal your moments, which means you'll miss out on a whole lot-o'-joy.

Here's what I mean by "steal your moments." Last year I went through a rather odd time of transition. Rather than taking off without makeup to run to Wal-Mart, as I've always done, I turned into the clone of a seventeen-year-old girl, only with a few more wrinkles and a lot more anti-aging cream.

Also, like a teen, I started spending more time in front of the mirror primping, fixing, smoothing, and shaping and wondered what I would do when I turn totally gray. Unfortunately, I also spent far too much time complaining about my age since I was just around the corner from the big "four-oh!" I imagine those closest to me noticed a new insecurity about my age creeping into my conversation, but they weren't the only ones taking notice.

God noticed too.

There are times when I know I hear Him speak into my spirit; other times I'm not sure. But one afternoon during this bout of "time of transition," as I like to call it, it was clear God wanted my attention. It was one of those moments when He caught me off guard; I wasn't expecting His voice. Just as I bowed my head to pray, He beat me to the punch with a rebuke: *I want you to stop complaining about your age. You're stealing my moments.*

Ouch.

I knew exactly what He meant, but the Holy Spirit went on to provide extra-added interpretation:

Shana, these are my moments that I've given you. When you're complaining about how old you are, you're looking back to the past in regret and despairing of the future. If you're longing for something you used to have, you're not embracing my now. Therefore, you're stealing the moments I've created—those that I'm working in.

In the same way that my complaints about my age chained me to the past and prevented me from experiencing the joys of the present, not letting go of unanswered questions about the past does so also.

There's a gentle balance between grieving the past well so that we can move on to greater maturity and hope—and holding onto the past and *refusing* to move on. Sadly, I did the latter, and it created heartache and pain.

In the classic book *Man's Search for Meaning*, Viktor E. Frankl, an Auschwitz survivor and psychologist, addresses the question as to why some prisoners survived the brutalities of life in a concentration camp while others did not. Certainly some were so ill they couldn't go on, but the distinguishing characteristic, says Frankl, was that those who looked to the future in hope lived. These courageous souls did not look backward and demand answers. Instead, they had "rich intellectual lives." They used their imaginations to plan the future. They thought about the joy that would be theirs when they saw their loved ones again, fulfilled a great purpose, or did something redemptive for humanity.

If we refuse to relinquish our questions about the past and demand answers about things we can't change, we'll miss out on the joy of today and hope for the future. Spending life looking through the rearview mirror brings emotional pain. Regretting the past and fearing the future brings torment.

Granted, sometimes we need to take a close look at the past and grieve it so that the Holy Spirit can heal us with His balm of truth. We may even need to speak with someone who can counsel us or pray us through our heartache and unanswered questions. However, there will come a time when we have to let go of what we'll never understand—and that time *will* come.

What I don't know about the past will most likely never be answered this side of heaven. There are still times when Satan throws my past up in my face to make me doubt myself, God's sovereignty, and His love so that he can pull me into a pit of self-pity. If he can make me dwell on questions about the past, he can make me think I've never overcome it, which he can use to destroy what God wants to do in my life. I know that if I want to move forward in peace and confidence, I can't allow my mind to spin into "what ifs." Otherwise, I'll end up in a hole of despair. I have to stop myself from rehashing and reevaluating what's long past and will never change. I have to choose to look forward.

When questions about the past and what you won't ever understand accost you, the best way is to live in the moment, embrace the mystery of God, and quiet your soul—as David did.

Still and quiet your soul to experience peace.

Because David knew that some things are "too wonderful" to understand about life and God, he chose not to worry about the things God had reserved to be mysteries. "I do not concern myself with great matters or things too wonderful for me," he wrote in Psalm 131:1.

Because he knew God was wonderfully mysterious, David chose to master his own soul—or mind. "But I have stilled and quieted my soul," he continues; "like a weaned child with its mother, like a weaned child is my soul within me" (verse 2).

"Stilling and quieting" one's soul is a choice; it's centering on the believing, silent parts of ourselves, pulling it into a quiet closet, away from pain-filled questions where we commune with God from a position of belief.

I did it at 3 A.M. this morning. When I couldn't sleep, I curled up into a fetal position with my head pointed toward my belly button and pulled the covers over my head. I spoke to God. I did not ask Him questions about my current trials or demand that He tell me why. Instead, I confessed my love for Him and asked a question of surrender: *Lord, will you help me to love you more?*

In those quiet moments, a sweet peace settled into my soul, a peace I imagine David experienced. When we choose to believe, and we let go of what we'll never understand, we embrace the magnificent mystery of God, and our unanswered questions melt away in the light of His sovereignty and love.

In the King James Version of Psalm 131:2, the word used instead of "stilled" in this passage by David is "behaved." I couldn't help but giggle about this. Sometimes it's a choice to make our souls—or minds—behave! Like an unruly child, we can tell our minds to sit down, shut up and obey God! (See 2 Corinthians 10:5.)

When questions of distrust torment us, we can still and quiet your souls by agreeing with God and His truth. For example, if we feel the urge to ask, "God, don't you love me?" we can make our souls behave by mentally embracing the truth that God does indeed love us—according to His Word. By replacing the lie-filled question with God's truth, we'll experience peace. If we want to ask, "God, why are you punishing me?" focus on the truth that God does not punish those He loves but that His discipline is always done in love (Hebrews 12:8-11).

I realize that thinking about all this bossing our minds around sounds exhausting; and it can be difficult at first. But as our minds are renewed through learning the truths in the Bible, it becomes a lot easier. This is why it is so critical to spend time alone with Christ and allow Him to speak to us about our lives and circumstances by communing with Him through prayer and meditating on His Word.

Take heart! There will come a time when all our questions will be silenced once and for all.

Make a list of questions, and laugh.

Are you disappointed because there's no guarantee that God will answer your questions this side of heaven? If so, perhaps you've decided to store some of your inquiries in the back of your mind for the time when you see Christ face to face in heaven. Like many people, maybe you've thought, *When I get to heaven, I'm going to ask God . . . why my husband left me. . . why my sister rejected me. . . why my house burned to the ground. . . why I miscarried.*

I have good news: There won't be any pain-filled questions in heaven.

When Jesus comforted His disciples in John 16:22-23 before His crucifixion, He acknowledged that they would be grieved but that He would return, and like a mother who had given birth, their labor pains of grief would be replaced by joy. He also said that "in that day, you will no longer ask me anything."

When we reach the glorious gates of heaven to meet Christ, all our questions about personal heartbreak will melt away. I'm not sure if it's because we'll all be like tongue-tied school girls in His presence or if it's because everything will finally make sense due to the fullness of the Holy Spirit (1 Corinthians 13:12). Either way, we won't be asking. No more struggling, wrestling, worrying, or wondering—just blessed peace.

Questions for Reflection

1. What is your initial response to this chapter?

2. What about it impacted you most?

3. What questions of belief have you asked God during times of trouble? Why?

4. Have you considered that your questions will diminish as God heals your heart?

5. What questions of distrust have you asked God during times of trouble when you haven't gotten something you hoped for?

6. How do you feel knowing that there are some questions that won't be answered this side of heaven?

7. How do you feel knowing that you won't have any questions in heaven?

Action Point

Make a list of the unanswered questions you have about your life. Then talk with God about them, thanking Him that one day in heaven all your questions will vanish.

10
God's Motives Can Be Mysterious

Life is God's novel. Let him write it.
—Isaac Bashevis

My mother talks in details. If you meet her, she probably wouldn't tell only that she purchased fabric for her latest wall hanging. Instead, she'll tell you *why* she purchased the fabric, *who* she was with at the store, *when* she did it, and *how much* it cost.

She might say something like "You know Mary? She's my neighbor who's married to the plumber, and she has the schnauzer named Skittles. Anyway, I went shopping with her today for two hours, and I purchased some fabric from the store around the corner from Judy's house. You remember Judy, right? Well, the fabric has a sort of blue background with an orange pattern running through it. I just love patterns. I make a lot of quilts using them. You should try it. Anyway, the fabric was on sale. Three dollars and ninety-nine cents per yard. Great deal!"

I recently learned from a radio program that my mother is a "circular communicator." She starts with a topic, talks in a circle while adding details, and then in conclusion she ties all the information together in a verbal bow.

When you were disappointed from losing something or someone, did you wish that God was more like my mom—giving details and spelling things out? I have. Although what God wants from us during hardship may seem like a mystery, there are things we can know about what He wants from us during times of trouble.

God wants to be first on your list of desires.

Imagine that a man knocks on your door and your husband answers. The man says, "Hey, I really like the way your wife looks. I'd like to take her home for the night to be with her, but I'll bring her back tomorrow."

How do you think your husband would respond? Would he say, "Okay, but make sure you have her back in time to make my breakfast"?

Fat chance.

Maybe he wouldn't say a thing, but he might punch the guy in the nose. Why? Because a man who loves his wife doesn't want to have to compete for her devotion; he wants to keep her all to himself.

God doesn't want to have to compete for your devotion either. Because you're the greatest desire on His list, He wants to be the greatest desire on yours. This isn't because He's bossy or controlling, but because He knows that when you love Him more than anything or anyone, you're protected against Satan's attempts to ruin your relationship with Him and destroy your life by making you believe God has betrayed you. Your love for God is a powerful weapon against roots of deception.

Maybe you're thinking, *Okay, I want to put God above everything else, but I don't know how.* Rest assured—it's not all up to you. Yes, God wants you to be willing, but He wants you to love Him more than you want to. For this reason, He'll nurture your relationship with Him through good times and bad.

There are two ways Christ can move to the top of your list of desires: one is by getting everything on your list, and the other is not getting everything you want.

King Solomon knew what it meant to get everything he desired: women, wine, adventure, and all the money he could want. His heart still felt empty. (See Ecclesiastes 2.) All his earthly desires were met, but he learned that nothing but God could truly satisfy.

Paul, on the other hand, was shipwrecked, stoned, and mocked. In his need and greatest moments of desperation, he found God faithful and worthy to be the greatest desire in his life (Ephesians 3:8-9). Because God loves us deeply, He'll use whatever means necessary to bring us to the end of ourselves so that He'll take His place at the top of our list.

Has God ever topped your list if only in a moment of desperation like Paul's? How about after you chased a dream that you were certain would deliver satisfaction only to find that it didn't, like Solomon?

Allow your pain to move you closer to Christ.

Several years ago I interviewed Heather Gemmen for an article I was writing. As with Paul, Christ had become her all—not in spite of tragedy but *because* of tragedy. As with most women, her husband and family held a place of prominence on her list. She was married and had three children. Life was good.

Then she got something she certainly didn't want.

One evening when her husband was away at church, Heather put her children to bed and turned in early. A short time later, someone entered her room. She thought it was her husband. "Turn out the light," Heather murmured. When she looked up, she saw a strange man standing in her bedroom. A nightmarish experience followed.

Afterward, Heather phoned her husband. It felt impossible to admit what had happened. Shame engulfed her as she spoke: "I've been raped!"

Even though Heather had been pro-life for years, she wasn't sure what to do. Overwhelmed by the thought of pregnancy, she took the morning-after pill after counseling by her pastor and Bible study group. She missed her period once or twice but was told it was stress-induced. Then she took a pregnancy test. The drug hadn't worked. Heather was pregnant. Confusion, fear, shame, and anger followed.

Heather traveled through heartache and came out the other side. When I asked her how the experience affected her relationship with God, she said that she has a deeper love for Him and confidence that He is Provider and Sustainer. She chose not to believe that God had abandoned her. "There are a lot of tough things that happen in life, but God is good," she said. Heather is a recipient of the abundant life in Christ because she has chosen to trust Him. She even wrote a book called *Startling Beauty* to tell the world how God turned her tragedy into blessing. Christ is at the top of Heather's list.

You might be wondering what happened to the baby. After navigating a maze of questions, Heather and her husband decided to keep little Rachel and love her. That's just like God.

Christian musician and singer Tammy Trent also experienced personal tragedy. As described earlier in this book, her husband, her high school sweetheart, died in a free diving accident in the Blue Lagoon in Jamaica on September 10, 2001. The next day, which happened to be 9/11, no planes were flying, and thus she couldn't get home. She was all alone.

In her book *Learning to Breathe Again*, Tammy writes that she lay on the bathroom floor of her hotel room and wailed. "I sobbed and moaned and cried so loudly the hard-tiled walls of the bathroom seemed to echo every sound."

In the midst of her pain, Tammy somehow mustered the courage to pray: *God, I'm not asking for a hundred angels; I'm just asking for one special angel, just one angel who could hold me right now. God, you're so big. . . if you can hear me, if you care. . . please do this for me.*

Tammy got up and looked out the bathroom doorway. A Jamaican woman, a housekeeper with a concerned look on her face, came in the room and said, "Oh! I've been trying to get to you. I could hear you crying. I've been trying to get to you." She paused and stepped toward Tammy. "Could I just come in and hold you?" she asked.

Tammy bit her lip and nodded. The woman wrapped her arms around Tammy as she leaned in, dropped her head on the woman's shoulder, and cried. God showed up in the middle of Tammy's desperation by sending her an angel in a housekeeping uniform. Through her grief, God has become more real to Tammy, and He tops her desires in a greater way than ever before.

When we're hurting, God may not send us an angel as He did for Tammy, and we may not hear Him speak audibly, but he does want to comfort us in our desperation to make himself more real to us. Through our pain He wants to top our list of desires. Psalm 34:18 says, He is "close to the brokenhearted and saves those who are crushed in spirit."

When Christ is your chief desire, He can redeem your trial.

As with many women, one of the deepest piercings of my heart centers around denied parental love. Because my father was never emotionally available and has passed away, I never was granted one of my desires—a close relationship with my dad. It will remain unchecked until I get to heaven.

In his book *The Journey of Desire* John Eldredge talks about "disowning desire"—pushing it down and denying what we long for most because we're not sure we're going to get it.

Is that what I should do with this God-given desire that hasn't disappeared, even though my dad is gone? Do I try to shove it down, kill it, or hope it disappears? Doing so seems impossible, especially since it's been woven into the fabric of my heart by the hand of God. It's part of who I am. It's innate, part of being human.

About a year after my dad passed away, I wrote a short reflection in my journal about him:

I miss my dad. It's strange how you can miss someone you never felt very close to. But I still miss him, because he was my father. I wish he was here so I could hug him and say, "I'm sorry." Sure, he didn't love me best, but I didn't love him best either.

Tears run down my cheeks now, and my heart hurts for what never was—a close relationship with my father. It's God-given that the human heart longs for parental love. If we don't receive it, we can spend a lifetime looking for it in success, money, accomplishments, another person's face, or a host of other things. We may deny that we ever needed or wanted it in an effort to deal with the pain of that lost love. After all, it's easier that way.

As a very tenderhearted child, I probably learned how to, as John Eldredge says, "disown my desire" for my dad's love, because I eventually learned that he would never provide me the protection and love I longed for. At some point in my journey I stopped hoping, because it was easier not to hope than to hope in pain. After all, hope breeds prayer, and prayer breeds expectation, and, as Proverbs 13:12 says, "Hope deferred makes the heart sick." Being heartsick hurts, so I stopped hoping for my dad's love. It was easier not to expect it than to be repeatedly disappointed.

Today I wonder if I missed something in my reflection. Is that all there is, that I resign myself to being heartsick until I go to heaven because I didn't get what I needed growing up? Or can something redemptive and beautiful happen for me when my desires are unfulfilled?

God longs to bring healing and wholeness to our lives. When I'm willing and keep Christ at the top of my list, the thing in my life that has caused the greatest emotional pain can be the very reason I experience my greatest redemption of heart. My most devastating losses can push me into deeper relationship with God; I can cry out to Him, and He can hold me in His bosom of grace.

That's beauty for ashes, joy for mourning, praise for despair (Isaiah 61:3).

When Christ is at the top of the list due to blessing or tragedy, He'll redeem the trial, and we'll experience the second thing he wants to give us—*zoe*.

God wants to give us *zoe*, the highest blessedness we can know.

A friend once called me and expressed how lonely and frustrated she was that God hadn't delivered the top desire on her list: a husband. Never married and now forty, she was tired of praying and waiting. Most of all, she was convinced that her life was somehow "less-than."

"Being single is *not* the abundant life," she stated emphatically.

I identified with the emotions of feeling like the only girl without a date to the high school prom. I empathized with her loneliness, her cries late at night when only God can hear, and a zillion prayers for a man she isn't even sure exists. But the absence of abundant life? I've felt that way, but that was before I knew God could be my all in all.

Our conversation sent me running for my Bible, where I found John 10:10—

> The thief comes only to steal and kill and destroy; I have come that they might have life, and have it to the full.

The word "life" jumped off the page. I *had* to look up its meaning. I pulled out my *New Testament Word Study Bible* to find the definition. In it I found the prescription for my friend's sickness of heart: God *himself* is the abundant life she seeks. The word "life" is the Greek word *zoe* (the original language) and means—

> "Life," referring to the principle of life in the *spirit and the soul*. [Zoe is] all the highest and best that Christ is, which He gives to the Saints. *The highest blessedness of the creature* (emphasis added).

This abundant life is internal—in the spirit, in the soul, God-given, the highest blessing we can receive. This abundant life is Christ himself!

How many times have we heard preachers talk about abundant life as if it's to be apprehended through something external, like our possessions, accomplishments, or something else on our list of desires? Instead, Christ says, "This abundant life that you're looking for—*it's who I am, it's internal, and it's found through relationship with me. If you'll let me, I'll run circles around any hope, dream, or desire on your list.*"

Because we have little control over our lives, isn't it a comfort to know that abundant life is not "out there" somewhere, but it's a gift of God?

This abundant life in the spirit and the soul is what inspired Paul to write about God from a prison cell, and it's what moved the psalmists and numerous other saints to praise in the midst of loneliness, starvation, destitution, and even sin.

When we know that He is life, and we've found satisfaction in Him, He tops our desires. We become willing to give up many things—including the dreams, hopes, and desires that we thought we could never be fulfilled without.

This abundant life through relationship with Christ is the reason Paul was willing to give up everything he considered valuable:

> Whatever was to my profit I now consider loss for the sake of Christ. What is more, I consider everything a loss compared to the surpassing greatness of knowing Christ Jesus my Lord, for whose sake I have lost all things. I consider them rubbish, that I may gain Christ and be found in him (*Ephesians 3:7-9*).

Paul had nothing on his list that surpassed knowing Christ—nothing.

If we have things on our list of desires that we consider to be better or more important than knowing Him, we leave ourselves vulnerable to Satan, causing us to feel betrayed, which can bring destruction to our relationship with God.

Keeping Christ at the top of the list can be challenging.

I wish I could say that once Christ tops the list, He stays there without any competition for the rest of our lives, always giving us *zoe* and redeeming heartache. Life would be a lot easier.

But we're prone to chase dreams, hopes, and desires that take priority over Him. Right now there are other things vying for first place on my list. I didn't mean for it to happen, but it did. I got distracted—a crisis hit. The next thing I knew, I was wandering around in a spiritual desert, looking for abundance from other people and other circumstances.

My cell phone bill provides a clue to my predicament. Life's challenges have led me to call and seek advice from my girlfriends. I've called Jamie, Sarah, Melonie, Judi, Linda, Jennifer, Tressa, and Kathleen—repeatedly. Because they love me, they want to help. But as you might have guessed, they all have their own ideas of what I should do. There's no long-term satisfaction or peace in that.

Unfortunately, several weeks passed before I remembered that my sweet girlfriends, as wonderful as they are, can't take the place of Christ. He's the only place to find answers and the abundance I've been looking for. So I've decided to take Joyce Meyer's advice and "Go to the throne, not to the phone."

Let me assure you: it *is* possible to find abundant life in Christ. I've been with it and without it. And right now I'm running back to Him with everything I have. When I get back to the arms of my only true love, I'll find His name, once again, scrawled across the top of my list. No chance of believing God has betrayed me then—and that's exactly where I want to be.

Remember that regardless of the trials we face, there are questions we must answer: What will we do with our pain? Will we allow it to draw us closer to God, or will we allow it to destroy our relationship with God? How we respond to these questions will determine our joy.

Questions for Reflection

1. What in this chapter spoke to you most?

2. Have you ever had a difficult time sharing honestly with God about your positive and negative emotions? If so, does it change your perspective to know that honesty is necessary for the healing of your heart?

3. Have you ever experienced a time in life when relationship with Christ has topped your list because of difficulty—like Paul or Heather?

4. Have you ever been blessed with something that topped your list and then discovered that it didn't satisfy?

5. What's your response to learning that God wants to give you *zoe*, abundant life that's internal and is not based on your circumstances?

6. Are you willing to surrender what's on your list of desires, even though you may not understand what God is doing in your life? Why or why not?

Action Point

Go to the Internet or your Bible's concordance, and look up the words "love," "lovingkindness," "affection," "grace," and "mercy." Then commit to memorizing two scriptures that speak to you about how God feels about you.

11
Heartbreak Can Threaten Your Relationship with Christ

God always trumps Satan.
—Beth Moore, *Esther: It's Tough Being a Woman*

The presence of evil is the strongest argument reason poses against faith.
—Ed Gungor, *What Bothers Me Most About Christianity*

A man's own folly ruins his life, yet his heart rages against the Lord.
—Proverbs 19:3

Dear friends, do not be surprised at the painful trial you are suffering, as though something strange were happening to you. But rejoice that you participate in the sufferings of Christ, so that you may be overjoyed when his glory is revealed.
—1 Peter 4:12-13

My grandmother once told me that during the time of log cabins, before hospitals, family members died at home. If you've ever been around someone who's at death's door, you know that the smell of death often precedes death. Grandma said that when this smell caught the attention of wolves, they crouched, scratched, and howled at the door of the cabin, trying to get in.

When a woman feels as if part of her heart has died because she hasn't not gotten something on her list or she got something she didn't want, Satan crouches at the door of her heart like one of those wolves Grandma told me about, ready to attack and drive a wedge between her and God by causing her to believe that He's betrayed her. When our hearts are broken, we can be very vulnerable to Satan's enticements to turn from Christ.

When we suffer the loss of something we want, or when life hands us a hardship we don't want, we may feel as if Satan has come after us in full attack mode. *Why has Satan made me his target? Why is he beating me up? And why does he even care to turn me against God?*

These are important questions, and I want to share several life-giving answers.

You have extreme value to God.

Satan crouches at the door to make us believe that God has betrayed us.

In his book *When I'm Longing for God,* Dan Stuecher tells a touching story about the great composer Beethoven. The music man never married but was in love with a woman scholars have spent years trying to identify, a woman Beethoven called his "Immortal Beloved."

When he was forty-two years old, Beethoven penned a letter of affection to her. "Oh, why must one be separated from her who is so dear?" he wrote. "However much you love me—my love for you is even greater."

After his death, the letter was found in a bureau belonging to Beethoven, undated and unaddressed. Some people have wondered if the woman ever knew how valuable she was to Beethoven because of this secret, undelivered note.

God's love for us is no secret—and Satan knows it. That's the reason he wants to come after you. Christ is shouting His love for us from the Cross, through the wonder of creation, and through the pages of Scripture so that we'll know without a doubt that He loves us madly.

- In John 15:9 Jesus announced the depth of His love for us when He said, "As the Father has loved me, so have I loved you." You are loved by Jesus as He is loved by His own Father!
- In Philippians 1:8 Paul noted that Christ's love is deep when he told the Philippians, "I long for all of you with the affection of Christ."
- In 1 John 4:10 the Bible says that God demonstrated His love by sending His son to die on the Cross for our sins. Do you know anyone else who would die for you? Now that's real love!

Numerous other scriptures describe God's love. Think about the significance of this for a minute. If a woman has an enemy she loathes and wants to destroy, would she attempt to ruin what her adversary *didn't* value? Of course not. To cut to the deepest part of her opponent's soul, she would want to ruin what her rival cherished most. In God's world, this is you. You top His list. God is in a battle for your affection because of *His* affection for *you*.

This battle is described in John 10:10—"The thief [Satan] comes only to steal and kill and destroy; I [Jesus] have come that they [you and I] may have life, and have it to the full." The semicolon indicates that the battle is going on between Satan and Jesus. What's all the fighting about?

You and me.

That's right. *We're* the object of the battle. *We're* the prize. This means that we must choose who we'll side with when Satan comes scratching at the door. Will we let him in by believing that God is a betrayer when we suffer loss or disappointment? Or will we choose to trust God?

A decision has to be made. Sorry. Jesus never said, "I want to give you life, and Satan wants to destroy you—but you can remain neutral if you want." Instead, he said as Joshua said, "Choose for yourselves this day whom you will serve" (Joshua 24:15). Because we're the battle prize, we don't have the privilege of standing on neutral ground. There really is no neutral ground in this matter.

I spoke with a young man who said he didn't want to choose a side in the battle. "I don't like thinking that I'm the object of battle; I like the idea that I'm just on my own—I'm in control up here," he said, pointing to his head with his index finger.

Right. I thought. *Why won't he acknowledge his part in the battle?* Then it hit me: when we know that God cares for us, believing that we're the prize in such a significant battle is a marvelous revelation of love. Imagine—God loves us enough to fight for us! We have extreme value to Him! However, if, like this man, we don't want to submit to God's authority, then admitting that we're the battle prize is uncomfortable, because it means that we must be accountable for our actions, our attitudes, our lives.

In God's economy we find not one independent human on earth; we all answer to someone—either God or Satan. Even though we may ignore the battle, it won't go away. We can't wish it away, and we can't pretend that it doesn't exist.

The question is—Whose side will we choose?

Take note that Ephesians 6:10 says that the way we do battle against the enemy is by putting on our armor, which involves truth, righteousness, faith, and trust in God's salvation. If someone doesn't believe Satan exists and doesn't trust God because of the belief that He has betrayed him or her, that means the person has no faith, which also means he or she isn't wearing a stitch of armor. Try to imagine people wearing their birthday suits into battle.

We're the recipients of God's promises.

Satan attacks us not only because we have extreme value to God but also because if he can get us to turn from Christ and believe He has betrayed us, then he can steal more than just what's on our lists of dreams, hopes, and desires.

Imagine I have a box filled with gold that I want to give you. Because I'm big on surprises, I drive to your home, ring the doorbell, and say, "Hey! It's your lucky day! I have a million dollars worth of gold in the trunk of my car. It's all yours, but you have to get it yourself."

At this point you would either believe me, think I was a liar, or assume I needed to take anti-loony medication. If you believed me, faith would propel you to retrieve your gift from my car. Of course, if you thought I was nuts or lying, you wouldn't bother.

Because God loves us, He wants to bless us with many precious promises that are described in the Bible. However, in the same way that you wouldn't get the gold if you didn't believe me, you won't receive these promises if you don't believe God and instead believe Satan's lies.

Granted, there are many unconditional promises in the Bible that can't be changed. They'll come about regardless of what we believe. For example, in John 14:3 Jesus said that He's coming back. This is a for-sure thing. It can't ever be altered, no matter what. In Hebrews 13:5 Jesus also said, "Never will I leave you; never will I forsake you." This is also an unconditional promise.

There are, however, *conditional* promises that Satan *can* prevent us from receiving if we side with him on the battlefield and let him through the doors to our hearts by believing God has betrayed us. Why? Because these promises can be apprehended only by faith, in the same way that one would get the gold only by believing.

For example, Philippians 4:6-13 contains a conditional promise. It says that we shouldn't be anxious about anything but instead should pray and ask God for what we need and then thank Him with faith for answering. As a result, peace will fill our hearts and minds. Note that peace is a conditional promise based on the faith demonstrated through prayer and thanksgiving.

If we believe that God has betrayed us, will we have the faith needed to receive this promise or others? Here are a few conditional promises that we can receive *only* by believing God.

- "Believe on the Lord Jesus, and you will be saved—you and your household" (Acts 16:31). Salvation is conditional, based on faith. How can we have faith in God if we're blaming Him for our heartaches?

- "Submit yourselves, then, to God. Resist the devil, and he will flee from you" (James 4:7). Ditching the devil is conditional, based on submitting to God. How can we submit to someone we don't trust?

- "Humble yourselves before the Lord, and he will lift you up" (James 4:10). Being lifted up is a conditional promise based on humility. How can we humble ourselves before someone we believe is unfaithful?

If Satan can convince us that God is a betrayer, he can cause us to abandon full faith, and that will get us on his side of the battlefield, where we'll miss out on many conditional promises. Not only that, but we'll also affect others negatively.

No woman or man is an island.

Having faith and not having faith are like having chicken pox—both are contagious. In the right doses and under the right circumstances, both can spread like wildfire to ignite others for good or to burn them. Although we like to think that our faith—or the absence of it—is a personal issue, it never is. What we believe *always* affects someone else, either for their benefit or their destruction.

If the devil can convince us that God is a betrayer who can't be trusted, then our spouses, children, in-laws, friends, neighbors, and acquaintances will be affected by our unbelief. If a woman believes that God has betrayed her, what *isn't* she telling her children about Jesus? If a woman buys into Satan's roots of deception, what *isn't* she sharing with her best friend that God loves her? If a man believes that God is a liar, what *isn't* he telling his wife about the Savior?

If Satan can seduce us into believing that God is a betrayer, he can deceive others through you. Contrary to what Simon and Garfunkel sang in the sixties, no man or woman is an island. No one is a rock that stands alone. We all affect one another. When my heart is filled (or not) with God, my lips will tell the story (or not) to others about His love (or lack of it). I am indeed my brother's (and my sister's) keeper.

Now that we understand that Satan wants to attack us because we have extreme value to God, that we're recipients of conditional promises and that what we believe affects others, let's look at some principles of Satan's battle plan to cause a woman or man to believe that God is a betrayer.

Satan is an opportunist.

Scripture says that after Jesus fasted for forty days and forty nights in the desert He was tempted by the devil: "When the devil had finished all this tempting, he left him until an *opportune time*" (Luke 4:13, emphasis added).

What is an "opportune time"? It's when circumstances and desire meet to fulfill a particular aim. This means that Satan doesn't randomly entice people to believe that God has betrayed them so they'll jump in a hole of sin. Instead, like the wolves I mentioned earlier, Satan's attacks are strategically made during crises, when our circumstances and his desire to ruin us meet, to fulfill his aim to cause us to believe that God has betrayed us.

This strategic attack plan of Satan's is found in the Old Testament Book of Job. It's important to note that Satan, like wolves, crouched at the door of Job's heart at just the right time. First, he destroyed many things on Job's list of dreams, hopes, and desires: his family, livestock, servants, and financial wealth. Then, when Job was at his lowest point, brokenhearted, and sitting alone in a pile of dust scraping himself with rocks, Satan suggested through Job's wife that he "curse God and die."

Satan's opportunities to tempt us to curse God can happen during financial, relational, physical, and emotional crises when we don't get what we want on our list or when we get something we don't want. They happen when uncontrollable circumstances invade our lives—when someone sins against us or someone else, or when we ourselves sin.

Satan uses three crisis opportunities to ruin our relationship with God by causing us to feel betrayed.

The crisis of uncontrollable circumstances. On August 30, 2003, Robert Rogers was traveling with his wife, Melissa, and their four small children from Wichita, Kansas, to their home in Kansas

City after a wedding reception. On the two-hundred-mile trip, the kids slept while Melissa drove. When they unexpectedly were caught in a flash flood on I-35, they were suddenly washed off the highway by a six-foot-tall wall of water.

Robert kicked out the van window, hoping to free his family. He was immediately sucked out of the vehicle into the water. He almost drowned but eventually surfaced and was washed to land. He was taken to a hospital for treatment of some minor scrapes— but his four children and his wife failed to make it out of the accident. They all drowned.

In the three days that followed, Robert identified the bodies of his four children and his beloved wife of eleven years. As he identified Melissa's body, the last of the five, his heart broke.

Robert recorded his thoughts in his moving book *Into the Deep*.

God, I need you as I've never needed you before, but Lord, I feel betrayed—as if you've built us up to tear us down. I'm so disappointed. I'm so let down. I don't feel as if I can trust you anymore. Everything you've given me, you've taken away. Why? For no reason you turned my world upside down. . . . I don't know if I can trust you now, Lord. I really don't know. I really don't want to. I really don't feel like trusting you anymore.

Robert experienced the vulnerability of being in the middle of a spiritual battle and losing what he loved so much, and Satan almost took advantage of his heartbreak in a circumstance he couldn't control. He was crouching at the door of Robert's heart, but Robert did not let him in.

Even though those thoughts were racing through my mind, I knew I would have to trust God, if for no other reason than because past experience and simple obedience told me to.

Robert later writes that in the aftermath of the accident, he made a conscious, active decision to turn to God after the death of his family.

> It felt risky to willingly place my trust in a God who had seemingly just betrayed my entire lifetime of trust; it rebelled against every fiber of reasoning and logic in my being. It was one of the hardest things to do as a man. Yet in "losing" my life to God—giving Him absolute control—I regained it. In dying to myself, He gave me life again.

Although Robert faced a circumstance that he couldn't control, and Satan made it seem that God couldn't be trusted and He had betrayed Robert, he chose trust.

The crisis of sin committed against us or someone else. Sin committed against us can also be an opportunity that Satan leverages to cause us to believe that God is a betrayer. Sin can be committed against us by one person or many. For example, it can be personal—such as a child who disowns us or a father who sexually abuses us—or it can be corporate in nature, such as a leader who deceives to seduce his followers into destruction. No matter what kind of sin is committed against us, whether it's personal or corporate, it can be used by the Satan to make us believe that God is a betrayer. We can even be led to believe that God can't be trusted when someone else has been sinned against.

For example, I recently spoke with a man who said his wife had seen a nine-month-old baby who had been beaten so badly that she sustained brain damage. This sweet little girl constantly cries; her vocal chords are raw. Tears, the language of her soul, have taken the place of words that can't be uttered. When I heard the story, my heart grieved. The man told me that his wife asked, "How could God allow something so horrible to happen? How could He allow someone to do that to that precious baby?" She was really asking, *God, are you fair? God, are you good? God, can you be trusted? God, are you loving and powerful?*

Sin that is committed against us or others, corporately or personally, can be used by the devil to make us feel betrayed.

The crisis of our own sin. We can also feel betrayed by God because of our own sin. The man who's an alcoholic and beats his wife and then loses her may blame God for allowing him to do the wrong thing. The woman who betrays a close friend through gossip may blame God for not intervening to stop her from speaking.

No doubt facing our own sin can be difficult. To admit that it wasn't an uncontrollable circumstance or someone else's sin that kept us from receiving what we wanted or dreamed of can be crushing. Humility and a teachable spirit are necessary during times of crisis when we sin. If we don't possess these qualities, Satan will make the most of this opportunity and cause us to blame someone else—and that someone could be God.

Satan promises relief from our crisis to seduce us to turn from Christ.

In Luke 4:1-13, when Jesus was experiencing the physical crisis of fatigue as well as facing the spiritual and emotional crisis of death on the Cross, Satan tried to cause Him to turn away from God by promising relief from the crisis in exchange for obedience. Satan took Jesus up to a high place so He could see all the kingdoms of the world. There he offered Jesus a shortcut to world domination without going through the Crucifixion, without obeying His Father: "I will give you all their authority and glory" (verse 6). "So if you worship me, it will be all yours" (verse 7).

When we experience crises from losing something we cherish or desire or getting something we don't want, Satan may come in with a promise to relieve us from our pain if we'll turn from

Christ—if we believe that He has betrayed us. Don't fall for it. Nothing is worth taking a shortcut around pain to get fast relief.

We can prevent Satan from taking advantage of us in times of crisis by doing what Jesus did in the wilderness: resist Satan with scripture. Three times Satan tried to deceive Jesus, and three times Jesus defended himself against deception with truth. He resisted the devil, and the devil fled (James 4:7). This is what is required of you and me when Satan comes at us during times of crises to tempt us to turn from God. We must battle him with truth. Today I got a cartoon via e-mail that read, "Greater is He who is in me than he who comes *at* me." Amen to that!

I recently saw an SUV with a bumper sticker that read, "Freedom isn't free." This proclamation was referring to the brave men and women serving our country in the military, but the same sentiment applies to us who desire to mature in Christ and experience more spiritual and emotional freedom.

Beth Moore has experienced freedom at a cost firsthand. When someone asked her how she gained the maturity and victory she currently has in life, she thought about it for a moment and then responded, "Disaster."

In Romans 5:3-4 God confirms Beth's sentiments: "We also rejoice in our sufferings, because we know that suffering produces perseverance; perseverance, character; and character, hope."

It seems like an upside-down way of looking at life, doesn't it? Trouble ultimately produces hope. Suffering leads to greater character. Disaster leads to maturity. Attacks from Satan lead to strength. Why? Because freedom isn't free. It's typically paid for and bought with pain, problems, and crises that make us want to throw up our hands and scream.

So what should our response be? We rejoice. How is it possible to rejoice in our sufferings? We must have the confident hope that something good is coming from our turmoil. We must choose to believe that a greater freedom is on its way, not in spite of the troubles we're experiencing but because of them.

Examine Your Heart

1. What did you find helpful in this chapter? Did any part of it bother you? If so, what?

2. How does it make you feel to learn that you're the object of the battle described in John 10:10? Do you relate more to the young man who didn't like the idea of being in the center of this fight, or with the idea that being the object is evidence of God's deep love?

3. How can you choose to side with God in the battle on a daily basis to prevent feelings of betrayal?

4. Have you ever considered that some of God's promises are conditional? What's your reaction to this truth?

5. What are some of the accusations that Satan has made to you about God or to you about yourself in an attempt to cause you to feel betrayed?

Action Point

On one side of a sheet of paper, list the benefits of following God and siding with Him in the battle when you don't get something you want or you get something that you didn't want. On the other side, write the disadvantages of siding with Satan. During the process, speak with God, and ask Him to show you His truth. When you're done, commit yourself to do His will, regardless of circumstances that make it seem that God is unfaithful.

12
Does God Care Enough to Make You Whole?

He will yet fill your mouth with laughter and your lips with shouts of joy.
—Job 8:21

God can heal a broken heart, but He has to have all the pieces.
—Author unknown

Hearts can be broken in an instant or slowly, over time. In an instant, like being bolted out of bed by an alarm clock, or slowly, like learning to speak French. Sometimes our hearts gradually break over a long season as we realize that a dream, hope, or desire isn't going to come to pass. Other times, breaking comes in a devastating blow—a moment in time.

In the aftermath of disappointment, when roots of deception cause us to discredit God, we may doubt that He wants to heal our hearts. To think that He would do so seems illogical, since we often see Him as the one who should have protected us in the first place. He said He would never leave us, but it seems that He abandoned us. He should have remained faithful, but it seems that He has betrayed us. Why would we think He cares to mend us?

Following are scriptural proofs that God wants to heal our broken hearts and reasons hearts may stay broken even though God wants to heal them.

There's proof that God wants to heal your heart.

God's on-purpose plan. Imagine that I telephone you and say, "Hey, could you come over? I need you to go to the grocery store for me."

Now imagine that when you get to my house you ask, "Okay, I'm ready to go. What do you need from the store?" and I respond, "Oh, I don't have a list for you. I just want you to go to the store."

How would you react? You would probably think that I had lost all my marbles, because it makes logical sense that if I'm going to send you on a mission, I would have a plan for you to accomplish something.

Now that we've established that it's nutty to send someone on a mission without a plan, we can be certain that God didn't send His Son to earth without a plan.

Scripture provides many explanations of why Jesus was sent to earth, but one of my favorites is Luke 4:18, where Jesus says, "The Spirit of the Lord is on me, because he has anointed me to preach good news to the poor. He has sent me to proclaim freedom for the prisoners and recovery of sight for the blind, to release the oppressed, to proclaim the year of the Lord's favor."

Isaiah 61:1 foretells, "He has sent me to bind up the brokenhearted." Jesus was sent on purpose, with an intentional plan to heal your broken heart!

Luke 19:41-44 gives us a moving insight of Jesus' reaction to those who didn't accept His coming to bind up the brokenhearted. "As he approached Jerusalem and saw the city, he wept over it and said, 'If you, even you, had only known on this day what would bring you peace—but now it is hidden from your eyes. . . because you did not recognize the time of God's coming to you'" (verses 41, 44).

Scripture says that Jesus wept. Can you imagine God Almighty, the Lord of heaven and earth, the maker of all things, the Alpha and the Omega, the Beginning and the End, weeping for humanity?

The original Greek text shows that the word "wept" is *klaio*, which means to "wail aloud." This word is different than what was used to describe Jesus' tears in John 11:35, which were silent. In contrast, *klaio* tears aren't quiet.

Why did Jesus wail? Because he loved the Jews, and He wanted to give them peace. He wanted to heal their hearts. But because they didn't recognize that God had come to them, they rejected Him and couldn't receive His blessings.

If Jesus wailed when the Jews rejected Him, can you imagine how He feels when He offers to bind up our broken hearts, and we reject Him and judge Him as a betrayer because we didn't get something in life that we wanted? How that must break His heart, especially considering the great sacrifice He made in dying for our sins—which leads me to the second scriptural proof that God wants to heal your broken heart.

Jesus' gift of love on the Cross. When I was in college, I visited my home church in southern Idaho to speak with my pastor. I was having a crisis of faith; I doubted God wanted to guide me in my personal life and career, and I felt lost, confused, and afraid.

The pastor gave me this analogy:

> Imagine that you had a daughter, and you loved her with all your heart. What if she came to you and said, "Momma, will you please give me a penny?" Would you become angry, yell at her, and tell her no? Absolutely not. Because you love your daughter, you would willingly give her something small like a penny, because you had already given her something as big as all your love.

Pastor went on to explain that God has already given me all His love in Jesus and His death on the Cross, and since He has done this for me, won't He also be willing to give me lesser things such as guidance and direction? In the same way, since God has already given us something as big as all His love in Jesus, it makes sense that He would be willing to give us something lesser, like healing for our hearts. If we don't believe so, then the love of the Cross has lost its magnitude, and we've made His love so small. Imagine how we would see God's desire to heal our hearts if we could grasp, as Paul says, "how wide and long and high and deep is the love of Christ" (Ephesians 3:18).

God sees your grief. In Psalm 10:1 Asaph asked, "Why, O LORD, do you stand far off? Why do you hide yourself in times of trouble?" When we believe that God doesn't want to heal our hearts, we'll feel that He doesn't see our grief. But nothing could be farther from the truth.

Even though Asaph wondered where God was, in verse 14 he embraced the truth and wrote, "But you, O God, do see trouble and grief; you consider it to take it in hand."

The word "grief" in this passage is the word *ka'as* in Hebrew. An amazing part of this word is that the most nominal forms of it involve the trouble that humanity causes, triggering hurt feelings. If we're experiencing grief from losing something we wanted or getting something we didn't want, there's likely more than just a few hurt feelings!

Thankfully, according to Asaph and the definition of *ka'as*, God notices all our heartache, overwhelming or small, and "takes it into hand," giving us assurance that He wants to heal our broken hearts.

There are reasons our hearts can stay broken.

Unforgiveness toward others: In the book *Tramp for the Lord* the late Corrie ten Boom tells a touching story. After her release from Ravensbruck, a Nazi concentration camp, Corrie traveled to Munich to tell her story of God's love and forgiveness to a room filled with Germans. During her speech, she told the crowd that God casts our sins into the ocean when we ask for forgiveness and that He remembers them no more (Micah 7:19).

Following her talk, a man approached Corrie. She recognized him as one of the cruelest guards in Ravensbruck. Immediately, pictures of her sister Betsie's slow and painful death at the hands of this man and others like him flooded Corrie's mind. When he reached Corrie, he said that he appreciated her message, then extended his hand. "How good it is to know that, as you say, all of our sins are at the bottom of the sea."

Corrie's arm stayed firmly at her side. She didn't want to shake his hand; she felt as if her blood had frozen in her veins. The man said he had become a Christian and knew that God had forgiven him for his cruel deeds, then asked Corrie, "Will you forgive me?"

She still didn't want to touch him. Her arms stayed by her side. But she knew that God calls us to forgive or we will not be forgiven (Matthew 6:15). She also thought about her own sins that God had forgiven and how those who nurse bitterness never overcome the past.

After a few seconds, Corrie remembered that forgiveness is not an emotion but rather an act of the will. *Jesus, help me!* she prayed. In obedience to God, she thrust her hand forward, even though she didn't feel like it. Immediately a warmth started in her shoulder and ran down her arm and into their joined hands. Jesus' love filled her heart and body. "I forgive you, brother," she said, "with all of my heart." Corrie wrote that she had never known God's love so intensely as she did then.

Forgiveness is powerful. It's a command. It's a choice. It's healing for a broken heart.

What would have happened if Corrie hadn't made the choice to forgive those who had wronged her and her family members? No doubt she would have remained imprisoned by the memory of Ravensbruck. Unforgiveness toward God and others would have stolen her ministry, testimony, confidence, and joy—and her heart would have stayed broken.

When we refuse to forgive others, something is always at work. Maybe we believe that God cannot or will not cause any good to come from what has happened or that something was taken that cannot be redeemed. Maybe we don't believe He can heal our heartbreak.

But when we acknowledge that He's all-powerful and that He loves us, He can make something beautiful out of the wrong that was done to us. When we choose to forgive, it pushes us to the edge of ourselves to make us more like Christ. Like Corrie ten

Boom, we can experience the redemption of wrongs committed against us when we forgive.

Envy. Envy can be a sign of feeling betrayed by God, and that can keep a woman's heartbreak fresh. When we see that God has given someone else what she has dreamed of or hoped for, we may wonder why He isn't doing the same for us. *After all,* we tell ourselves, *I've prayed more than she ever did, and I would be a better steward of that gift than she will be. Why, she isn't even following God!*

When we feel someone is undeserving, isn't there something in us that wants to scream, *God! What are you thinking?*

I recently caught myself thinking that way when I noticed a young couple embracing at the table next to mine in the coffee shop. They gazed into each other's eyes, and their lips locked as they waited for their lattes. I had to look away as raindrops of grief pelted my soul. *Look at what they have, and look at me—I'm sitting here romancing my laptop and a white chocolate mocha.*

Thankfully, I didn't stay in self-pity mode long, because I know the truth: If a woman wants to experience an abundant life in Christ, there's no room for envy in her heart. Christ tells us that we can be content, because His presence is constant (Hebrews 13:5). If I want to stand strong in God while I grieve what I don't have, I have to choose to believe that God has a very personal plan for my life. This will keep me safe in God's love and free from the ongoing devastation of a broken heart. *Go ahead and smooch while I enjoy my coffee!*

Comparing ourselves to our neighbors can lead us into a pit of despair that feels impossible to escape. Today I spoke with a friend who confessed resentment toward a former roommate: "She's spiteful, mean, and condescending," she said. When my friend found out that her former roomie got something *she* wanted, she had to run to the ladies' room at work to cry. As she told me her story, she said, "She's so unkind, so if God is blessing her and He's not blessing me, I must *really* be evil." Shame-filled tears covered her cheeks. I wished that I could give her a shot of trust in God's love so that she could find peace and believe that He hadn't betrayed her.

Maybe you're wondering why my friend didn't get what she wanted and hoped for while her former roommate did. Of course, it has nothing to do with being good or bad, evil or righteous, as my friend believed. That's a lie. Granted, God does reward us for our obedience, and blessings come from following Him. However, no one gets everything she wants, and it's dangerous to measure our worth or God's love by our circumstances.

God is all about variety. Because you're uniquely created, the plan for your life requires a unique response from God. It would actually be unkind of Him to ignore your individuality and treat you just like your roomie, neighbor, friend, sister, or mother. He's painting a beautiful never-before-painted picture on the canvas of your life that He'll be working on until you go home to heaven.

Guilt and unforgiveness toward ourselves. When I was an elementary school teacher, one of my coworkers received red roses. I asked, "Ooo—who sent you the beautiful flowers?"

She sighed. "They're from my ex-husband. He cheated on me, and I divorced him two years ago. Now he feels bad about what happened, so every Friday for the last two years he's sent me a dozen red roses." Disdain filled her eyes.

My heart broke for my friend's ex-husband. He had been deceived into sin and hadn't forgiven himself, which had prevented his broken heart from healing. Perhaps he thought that only his wife's forgiveness could set him free from his guilt.

I empathized with this man, because I struggled with so much guilt. I once wrote in my journal that if I had lived during the time of Christ when stoning took place, I think I would have been the first person to figure out how to kill herself with rocks.

If you feel guilty for a wrong you've committed against someone else, take heart. Romans 12:18 says, "If it is possible, as far as it depends on you, live at peace with everyone." Sometimes, even though we've done "as far as it depends on you" and asked for forgiveness from the one we've hurt, he or she may not want to forgive—and all the red roses in the world won't help. No doubt this can be very painful. If we wish that someone would forgive us so that we can forgive ourselves, remember that God has already removed our guilt through Christ.

We can feel guilty for lots of reasons, not just for wronging someone. Any time we don't forgive ourselves, our hearts won't heal.

Perhaps you're asking, *How do I tell the difference between false guilt and real guilt?* False guilt leads to ruin, and conviction by God always leads to wholeness and healing. If we suffer from false guilt, we'll be chained to the past in regret, which, just like unforgiveness toward others, will keep my broken heart from healing.

I recently found an old journal with this quote:

> When I forgive myself, I can let go of the past, and therefore I open myself up to hope for the future. I stop feeling like the victim, and instead, I look to your love, Jesus. Then I no longer feel as if you betrayed me.

If we have broken hearts that won't heal because we can't forgive ourselves for past wrongs we've committed, we can take that guilt to God and receive His forgiveness.

Blaming God: When we blame God, we've not submitted to His authority, sovereignty, or plan for our lives. When we believe the lie that He has wronged us, there will be no healing for our broken hearts. Why? Because authentic healing happens within the context of relationship with Christ—and it's impossible to have a good relationship with someone we are holding a grudge against.

When we're angry with God or believe He has let us down, we really have only two options when we're hurting: trust or torment. We can choose to trust God and let Him have His way, or we can be tormented by bitterness of heart.

A lack of hope for the future and holding on to the past. When we've lost hope that anything good will come to us in the days ahead, when we believe that the most beautiful part of our existence is behind us, we'll never be able to let go of the past to embrace the future, and our broken hearts will stay broken. The answer is to believe God and His personal plans for the days ahead.

Having a healed heart doesn't mean the things that have wounded us most deeply won't ever hurt again. Neither does it mean that God will get out His magic eraser to make it seem as if our troubles never happened. This side of heaven, brokenness is part of the human condition. It's also a condition God uses to reveal and glorify himself.

In our culture, brokenness is seen as a detriment, a subtraction to existence, but God says that He will not despise a broken and contrite heart (Psalm 51:17). A broken heart that has turned to Him is beautiful. But when we believe God has betrayed us, Satan is taking advantage of what has wounded us.

Remember: the healing of a broken heart is a "God thing."

Cooperate with God for healing, but know that it can't be done alone.

Many things can be accomplished by humanity—the study of the stars, building multi-million-dollar industries, cloning—but the transformation of the human heart is another story.

That alone is a *God thing*.

Those of us who have tried to change our fears, frustrations, anxieties, or addictions without Him know what I mean. Certainly we can cooperate with God for healing, but we're ultimately dependent upon Him to remake our hearts and heal our broken places.

I believe He likes it that way.

I think there are many reasons why, but one is that few things show us and the world His love as much as a heart that has been changed from fear to faith, hatred to humility, and bondage to believing.

In Ezekiel 36:26 God says, "I will give you a new heart and put a new spirit in you; I will remove from you your heart of stone and give you a heart of flesh." Notice that God says, "*I* will give." It's as if He's saying, "Child, no matter how hard you try, healing won't be a gift you give yourself. You can't manipulate it into happening or do it alone by working your own way to emotional and spiritual wholeness. You won't do it independently of me, because healing always happens within the context of relationship with me. *This*, dear one, is going to be of me, and it will be my work. Then, when you're healed, you'll know that I am the God who loves and saves you."

There were times when I wondered if my heart would ever heal; it seemed as if God wasn't doing a thing to help me get past my pain. Can you relate?

That's how life must look to the bird who sits on her nest. Things are apparently at a standstill. But the bird sits quietly, knowing that in the stillness something vital is going on and that in the proper time it will be shown. It takes faith and patience for the bird, and such faith and patience never seem to waiver, day after day, night after night, as she bides the appointed time.

Restless and doubtful, we wonder if the healing of our hearts will ever come, because we see no visible signs of progress. Let us remember the perfect egg, unchanged in its appearance from the day it's laid. But as the bird faithfully waits, doing the thing that she's supposed to do during those silent weeks, important things are happening and taking place.

And so it is with us. As we faithfully wait on God, doing what we're supposed to do—choosing to trust Him, choosing to believe during the silent weeks, perhaps even months and years—God is remaking our hearts!

It's as if the transformation and healing of our hearts were done in secret. How many times have I been clueless about His work in me until He revealed the finished product? Then, when I least expected it, He pulled back the curtain covering the place in my heart that was once wounded and exclaimed, "Look, child! See how I've healed you! Now you know it was all me."

Many times God's secret, transforming work has moved me to my knees, to tears, to gratitude. Who else but God? Who else but my Savior?

When we're frustrated because we want to see more emotional or spiritual progress and we want God to hurry and mend our hearts, we can trust, believe, wait, rest. He is transforming us.

Examine Your Heart

1. Is there something you sense God wants you to gain from this chapter?

2. What did you read that you relate to most?

3. What scriptural proof that God wants to heal your heart touched you the most? Why?

4. How does it make you feel knowing that Jesus wailed when those He wanted to heal, bless, and bring peace to rejected Him? What does this tell you about His heart toward us when we need Him most?

5. Which of the three reasons a broken heart won't heal speaks to you?

Action Point

If you feel that your broken heart has stayed broken for one of the four reasons listed in this chapter, write a letter to yourself, another person, or God. Write about the wrong—then give it to God in prayer. Ask Him to meet you in conversation and heal your heart. You may even want to hold your palms out and up in an act of surrender.

13
Getting Back to God

What we are is God's gift to us. What we become is our gift to God.

—Eleanor Powell

The greatness of a man's power is the measure of his surrender.

—William Booth

When I was seven, my mother heard from our neighbor that her two elementary-aged boys had chicken pox, so Mom suggested to my older sister and me, "Melonie and Shana, why don't you go play with Mike and Jerry?" We thought it was a good idea, so we happily bounced down the street, unaware of the red, itchy dots that would likely result from our visit. As we approached our neighbors' backyard, we heard our friends playing. Mike yelled at us, "You can't come back here! We're sick! We have chicken pox!"

Rarely deterred by danger, my sister yelled, "I don't care!" and climbed over the fence. But because I was afraid, I ran home to avoid illness.

My plan didn't work. But Mom's did.

My sister caught chicken pox and then gave the virus to me, just as my mother had hoped. Mom knew that once we caught the bug, we would become immune, and she wanted us to catch it while we were young.

I wish that feeling betrayed by God was like catching chicken pox—a one-time exposure means immunity forever. Unfortunately, because heartbreak and disappointment happen often in life, feeling betrayed and consequently falling into the trap of offense are both experiences we may repeat. That's why it's important to have a plan to overcome them.

Maybe you've heard that the first step to master a problem is to identify it. Hopefully, that's what the previous chapters have done. You've learned that deception plays an important role in feeling betrayed; looked at questions of unbelief; been shown how betrayal can lead to becoming offended, which causes behavior that leads to ruin; identified the results—or seeds of—betrayal, such as idolatry, hardness of heart, and making vows; and we've discussed how making God in our own image is a major component of believing God can't be trusted.

Now I want to give you some practical tools to help you hold tightly to Christ and avoid believing He's a betrayer and falling into the trap of offense when everything in you is screaming that He's been unfaithful, unfair, unloving, or unkind.

Make the choice to trust.

I recently heard a man say that the Christian faith is a crutch for weak-willed people who can't handle life on their own. I couldn't help but laugh, because any woman—or man—who has successfully walked through a valley of heartache knows that clinging to Christ when you would rather not, going God's way when you would rather be your own boss, and choosing to trust Him when you would like to tell Him to get lost is not for spiritual or emotional wimps.

In the same way, overcoming feelings that God is a betrayer is not for the faint of heart. It means making the choice to say no to Satan's lies and yes to God's truth—regardless of how much life hurts.

My friend Rick Webster is well-acquainted with the strength it takes to say yes to God. During a ski trip in West Virginia with his family in 2000, he had no idea that he would soon need to make the choice to trust God as never before.

When Rick's ten-year-old daughter, Emily, broke her leg on the slopes, he gently placed her in the back of their SUV so she could lie down during the drive home. Joni, Rick's wife, joined Emily in the back seat to keep her company; and later, for the first time, Rick and his wife agreed to allow their toddler, Gabriel, to ride unsecured in the back with them for the last few miles of the trip.

A half hour from home, Rick daydreamed about sending his children to a Christian camp when they were older—and that's the last thing he remembers. Approximately eight hours later, when he woke up in a hospital, he didn't know he had driven into a tree. He also didn't know that Joni, Emily, and Daniel had received massive head injuries and that they were all in critical condition.

Rick believes that God erased his memory about the accident because of His great mercy. "Otherwise, I would have suffered from a lot of guilt, and I'm certain I wouldn't have been able to handle it. I believe I would have ended my life."

The night after the accident, Gabriel went home to be with Christ. The next day, Emily followed her little brother to heaven, and Joni died that evening.

Amazingly, Rick chose not to believe God had betrayed Him. "It was definitely a choice," he says. "I had to ask myself, 'Am I going to turn away from God or am I going to draw near to Him?' I chose to draw near."

When I spoke with Rick about the tragedy that took his family, he said that in the months prior to the accident, he spent time in the mornings meditating on God's truth. The Lord reminded Rick of His love and about his identity in Christ. He is confident that this was critical to how he responded to the trauma. "Because I'd been spending time with God when the accident happened, my faith was driven into the bedrock,"—and like Christ in Matthew 4:1-10, Rick withstood the temptation to turn from his Father.

It quickly became obvious to Rick that God was in control of the accident and his life. "Even though I was devastated, I knew I had survived because God still had a plan for me, but my family's purpose on earth was done. God showed me that I didn't have to understand why He took Joni, Emily, and Gabriel. My job was to trust Him."

Because of Rick's humility and decision to trust, he experienced increased faith and hope rather than feelings of betrayal and despair. As suggested by Acts 14:22, the kingdom of God grew in Rick's heart through tribulation.

Like Rick, John the Baptist was also given the choice to trust Christ or to believe that God had betrayed Him and experience offense. When he was thrown into prison after paving the way for Christ's ministry, he became so disillusioned that he sent his disciples to verify Jesus' identity by having them ask if He really was the Savior. Jesus saw through John's question to his disappointment and feelings of betrayal. In response, He sent a powerful message back to John: "Blessed is he who is not offended because of Me" (Matthew 11:6, NKJV). In essence, Jesus was saying, "John, you have a choice to trust me or to become offended because of what's happening to you."

Just as it was for John the Baptist and Rick, you and I will inevitably come to many crossroads where we'll need to make the choice to trust God. The good news is that Jesus told John that blessings are available when we choose trust over feeling betrayal or falling into sin. Scripture also promises that those who hold unswervingly to hope, and who do not throw away their confidence, will be richly rewarded (Hebrews 10:23).

Of course, making the choice to trust doesn't mean we won't wrestle with painful emotions like confusion, frustration, and even anger.

Express your anger to God—it's a normal emotion.

In one of my former jobs I hung a poster outside my cubicle showing Lucy from *Peanuts* screaming, "Look out, everybody! I'm gonna be cranky for the rest of the day!" Lucy's announcement became a joke with my coworkers, because she's so *not* like me. I don't usually show anger.

In my youth I learned that anger was unacceptable, possibly because I often saw it misused. Then when I came to Christ, this faulty message was reinforced in church. After all, good Christian boys and girls never get angry, right? Wrong. Not only is this teaching wrong, but God *expects* that we'll experience anger. Jesus never said, "Don't get angry," but rather Paul instructs us to "Be angry, and do not sin" (Ephesians 4:26, NKJV). In this scripture He acknowledged that people would get angry. Why? Because anger is a secondary response to emotional pain. No doubt there's a lot of emotional pain to go around on this sin-filled planet. Anger *will* happen!

Like the questions we ask when we're hurting, anger is a red light on the dashboard of a car signaling that something's wrong under the hood—that there's a hurt we need to give to God, or perhaps forgiveness we need to grant someone. Anger also has the potential to take us to places of deeper intimacy with Christ when we bring our disappointments to Him for healing.

How can you do this? Yell or scream when no one is around, or run outside and holler. You can also do what author Muriel Cook calls "hot pen journaling." Write down your true emotions without sweetening them. Be real. Tell God the truth. Then ask Him to show you what's fueling your anger so He can minister to your pain through prayer and His Word to help you avoid becoming offended. Conversing with God about your anger thwarts Satan's plan to destroy your affection for Christ, because it keeps communication open with Christ.

Some time ago I was angry when someone I loved hurt my feelings. Rather than denying how I felt, sinning by taking it out on someone, or seeking revenge, I beat up my bed. I yelled. I screamed. I clobbered it as hard as I could. The result? I felt one hundred percent better. I forgave the person who wounded me and thanked God for loving me. Minutes later I was singing a song, proclaiming His truth and praising His name.

For some women, being real about their anger may sound sacrilegious. After all, aren't the most holy women composed and postured, even when the world and the devil walk all over them?

As I mentioned before, the psalmists, inspired by the Holy Spirit, were honest with God about their most raw emotions—including anger. To cry out in anger and anguish because life hurts is normal.

I'm not saying it's okay to mock God or treat Him with irreverence. Certainly there's a difference between taking your anger *to* God for healing and aiming your anger *at* God in defiance and rage. Taking your anger to God in humility means that you're operating in faith, that you feel safe enough to trust Him with your most uncomfortable and ugly emotions, and to approach His throne of grace with confidence to find mercy in your time of need (Hebrews 4:16). It also means you've opened your heart to Him in faith, knowing He has an answer for your disappointment.

But remember as you take your anger to Him to surrender to what you don't understand, and praise Him, too.

Praise Him when your "internal weather" is bad

One day last summer it was overcast—in the sky and in my heart. When I went for a walk near my home, the gloomy weather mirrored my mood. For some reason, I decided to find pictures in the clouds above me as I used to when I was little. However, when I started my game, everything I saw in the fluffy shapes looked mean; everything had teeth. It was as if a violent zoo had filled up the heavens. A handful of beasties snarled at me from above. *Great—that's just what I need,* I thought.

On my return trip home, I decided to praise God as an antidote to my cranky attitude. I thanked Him for bringing good out of things that were bothering me, for being in control, for loving me—and I told Him how awesome He is.

Suddenly the clouds—both internally and externally—were transformed. And wouldn't you know it? My next glance at the sky looked different! A laughing girl with pigtails came into view, then a happy hippo chasing a fish caught my eye. Suddenly the entire sky above me was filled with frolicking animals and at least a half-dozen giggling babies lying on their backs.

Oh! Joyous praise! When it filled my mouth, the nasty external—and internal—weather was changed.

This brings me to an important point about prayer: When we pray about what ails us and we revisit the heartbreak of not getting or of losing something we wanted badly, we must not just make requests to God—we should also give Him thanks. Why? Because thanksgiving is the "I believe" of prayer. If I pour out my anguish to God without being thankful, I experience despair; but when I thank God for what He has done and what He's going to do, I experience hope. I experience peace. This is the promise of Philippians 4:7.

So when we experience nasty internal or external weather, suffer heartbreak, and we're beating up our beds and doing "hot pen journaling," we must not forget to follow it up with a good dose of thanksgiving.

Keep eternity in mind.

A few months after my father died, I met him in a farmer's field scattered with carnival rides, craft tables, and food booths where he told me a secret about heaven. While I was surprised to see him, I wasn't surprised to see him *there*, because it was when he was happiest—barbecuing a side of beef, wearing an apron, toting a carving knife, and inviting small-town carnival-goers to sample his secret sauce.

At first, I couldn't believe it was him. When I saw him from the back many yards away, I thought, *That can't be Dad—he died!* Then as he strode toward me, excitement engulfed me. *It's him!* His smile beamed as the sun glistened on his wire-frame glasses. True to form, he wore socks that didn't match his shorts, and his legs needed to see more of summer. When he reached me, he smiled broadly and said, "Well, hi, Shana!" I was surprised that he acted as if he hadn't died and that no time had passed at all.

He placed his foot on the curb next to me and bent down to tie his shoe. I gazed at him in awe. I intuitively knew I would only have a short time to say what was most important to me, so I spoke quickly.

Because I wanted to thank him for his care, I said, "Dad, I want you to know that I took the money that you left, paid off all my bills, and I invested the rest of it."

He stood up, looked me straight in the eye, and grinned. "Well, Shana, I'm proud of you!" My heart melted. He said what I wanted to hear my entire life—he was proud. My chest ached with tears that wanted to flow but didn't.

Then he shared something I needed to know about eternity. "You know what I've learned?" he quipped. "I've learned that it really does matter in heaven what you do on the earth."

And then he was gone—quicker than he had come.

When I woke from my dream, my eyes filled with tears, and I quickly found my journal to record the message for a future time. That time is now. You see, my father's message wasn't just for me—it's also for you as you wrestle with disappointment.

Sometimes we think that nothing good can come from our heartbreak. But when we choose to believe God in spite of what has happened in our lives, Christ can use our stories to influence others so that they can go to heaven. Could there be any greater honor? Indeed, what you do on the earth—and specifically how you respond to your suffering—really will matter for eternity.

When we live in the hope of heaven, the ability to surrender to God what we don't understand increases, because we're aware that this life is just a dot on the timeline of all that God is doing. But we know that everything will make sense in heaven.

As a victim of childhood sexual abuse, Beth Moore grew from a shy, troubled girl who used to pull her hair out by the handful into an insecure woman who made many wrong choices. Beth could have blamed God and become bitter. But she didn't. Now she's a powerful communicator with an international teaching ministry that has reached more than 650,000 women in the United States alone through her Living Proof conferences. Women of many denominations and countries have completed her Bible studies. Who knows how many are being influenced for eternity because of Beth's obedience to trust God rather than turn away from Him because of heartache.

Like Beth and many other courageous women, God wants to use what has happened to us to influence others for heaven when we trust Him in spite of what has happened to us. Granted, we may not start a writing and speaking ministry, but every day our lives speak to others about the faithfulness of God as we trust Him in the midst of heartbreak. No doubt this can affect others for eternity.

Although it doesn't often seem like it, these are "light and momentary troubles" that will be outweighed by the glory of heaven (2 Corinthians 4:17-18).

Fight deception with the truth of God's Word, and prepare for battle in advance.

Many years ago when I was a teacher, I watched from an upstairs window at the school where I taught as paramedics arrived within minutes to rescue a man who had driven off the road. It struck me how different things were when I was a girl. Before electronic devices, such as global positioning systems (GPSs), paramedics had to know the city they served like the back of their hands, or else they would be driving around in circles in total chaos, and many people would have died! The paramedics had to know the city by heart so they were ready to respond when accidents happened.

In the same way, if we want to overcome the belief that God is a betrayer, it's critical to hide His truth in our hearts *before* personal devastation and disappointment hit. This will help to uproot the roots of betrayal. Otherwise, just like a paramedic who doesn't know the way, we'll panic and scramble, trying to find peace and direction. Those of us who have done it can testify that it's not effective.

When Jesus was tempted by Satan in the wilderness, after fasting for forty days and forty nights, He showed that the only defense against deception is God's truth. When Satan attacked Christ with lies, Jesus used scripture from the Book of Deuteronomy for protection. Can you imagine what it would have been like if He hadn't know the truth? It wouldn't have been a pretty picture if He had to stop and say, "Wait a minute! I have to go look that up! I think it's somewhere in the Scripture."

Like Christ, we can overcome the deceptions Satan throws at us to drive a wedge in our relationship with God. How? First, we can ask Christ what roots of deception we believe about Him, ourselves, our relationship with Him and His Word—or anything else that He wants to bring up about a particular heartbreak. Then we can make a list of the deceptions and ask the Holy Spirit to show us God's truth from Scripture. It's critical to know what God says about our circumstance in order to be free of feelings of betrayal and falling into offense.

One day while I was smack dab in the middle of a valley of weeping, I purchased some note cards and wrote a lie on each card with a counteracting scripture. I carried these scripture cards with me often and spoke God's truth out loud. Embracing His truth and choosing to believe Him was the beginning of a change in my heart and a movement away from believing God couldn't be trusted toward a place of peace and acceptance.

Give yourself time to heal, and fully trust God.

You've heard the old saying "Time heals all wounds." I wonder who thought of that one! Possibly it was someone who wanted to placate a friend who was going through a desperate time and needed some kind of hope to hold on to.

While time does give God a framework to work within, it heals nothing—only the power of God heals. This is important to remember as you move from believing God can't be trusted to peace and acceptance. Even though you've said yes to the healing of your heart and to God, it often takes time for Him to expose any roots of deception that have led to feelings of betrayal and possibly even to offense. Your job is to cooperate with Him and stay close by Him in the process. The good news is that no matter how long it takes to remake your heart, God will be working on your behalf.

So if you get frustrated on your way to spiritual and emotional wholeness because you want to trust God more but keep getting stuck in some of your old ways of thinking, be encouraged. Because He loves you and you're willing, God will transform your heart and mind.

Examine Your Heart

1. What did you like most about this chapter? What spoke to you most deeply?

2. How does it make you feel to know that believing God is a betrayer is a matter of choice?

3. Have you ever bought into the lie that it's not okay to express anger to God? If so, what contributed to that belief?

4. What are some practical things you can do to arm yourself with the truth in advance of your next heartbreak to protect yourself from feeling betrayed by God?

5. Have you ever panicked and scrambled in the midst of turmoil because you were unprepared to defend yourself against Satan's attacks with God's truth? What happened?

6. Healing of the heart takes time. Do you feel equipped to hang in there and wait on God?

Action Point

Find somewhere quiet, and write a note to God telling Him what's on your mind. Then ask Him to keep you close to Him during times of heartbreak in the future. Finally, praise Him that your healing is on its way!

Acknowledgments

This is painful. How do I fit onto one page the names of everyone who has encouraged and inspired me?

To my team at Beyond Imagination: where would I be without you? Thank you for believing in me.

To Elaine Proost: thank you for being faithful at the beginning. I'm where I am now because of you.

To my former colleagues at Focus on the Family: thank you for giving me so many opportunities to put words onto a page.

To my girlfriends Sarah Crawford, Tressa Johns, Jennifer Sugg, Kathleen Dalzell, Jamie Bell, Judy Dunn, Maxine Jackson, and Shari Martin: thank you for putting up with me!

To the Linklings: I appreciate your encouragement.

To Beth Moore: this book was birthed in my mind in a single moment as I sat on the front row of your Sunday School class. Thank you for inspiring me!

To my literary agent, Blythe Daniel: you're patient! How long ago did we start this project?

To my friend, Judi, who went home to heaven before the book's release: I miss speaking with you in an English accent. No one else gets it!

To my brother, Gannon, and my dad: Gannon, thank you for your support. I love you. Dad, you had a passion to write; now I do, too. One day, when I get to heaven, we'll share stories and poems.

To every unnamed friend who has inspired me with a kind word or action: thank you!

And to Jesus—my husband, my Counselor, my very best friend. This is your story. How could I have anticipated that something like this could come from feeling as if you had been unfaithful? Only *you* could do something so redemptive.

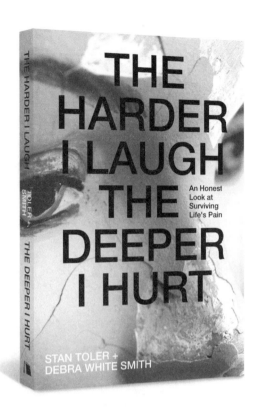

Behind the laughter and happy exteriors, **many of us are silently aching from the side effects of life's pain.** We believe in God's goodness, but sometimes we still struggle with the wounds of the past. In *The Harder I Laugh, the Deeper I Hurt,* authors Stan Toler and Debra White Smith explain how God used the healing gift of laughter to get them through their darkest moments. Their words of comfort and hope will help you **learn to let God's wisdom and peace heal your pain** with a joy that will remain genuine—even when life is at its worst.

The Harder I Laugh, the Deeper I Hurt
By Stan Toler and Debra White Smith
ISBN: 978-0-8341-2377-9

BEACON HILL PRESS
OF KANSAS CITY

Available online and wherever books are sold.

WHAT HAPPENS TO OUR FAITH WHEN OUR GIANTS DEFEAT US?

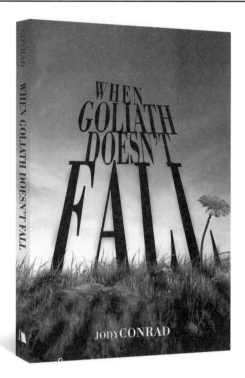

In this honest exploration of faith, author Jody Conrad pulls away the mask of Christianity and admits to the ugliness of real life. With compassion and understanding, she joins you in life's trenches and tells you about the unconditional and strangely hopeful worship of the prophet Habakkuk.

Her eloquent words and encouraging insights will lead you to a different kind of deliverance and will help you cultivate a beautiful, wild faith that still worships, still rejoices, still sings of the joys of heaven—even when Goliath doesn't fall.

When Goliath Doesn't Fall
By Jody Conrad
ISBN: 978-0-8341-2357-1

BEACON HILL PRESS
OF KANSAS CITY
